The Path to Cawdor

a Photographic Tour
with
Macbeth Connections

Written, Photographed and Published
by
Brian Lockey

ISBN - 13: 978-1515147091
ISBN - 10: 1515147096

Acknowledgements

I'd like to thank my wife Ann for her support and help in all aspects of this, my first book. Without her constant love and encouragement I would never have got started, let alone finish it.

Fiona Watson (see also the Introduction) was an inspiration. Her fascinating book about the real Macbeth changed my whole outlook and approach to this book. A simple collection of photographs with text turned into something with more meaning.

Alan, a great friend from school days, played a great part in encouraging me, especially at the beginning. He's had to suffer reading my early rough drafts as well.

I'm also grateful to favourite neighbours Graham and June, who cheerfully encouraged me, even after reading draft text supported by poor images on cheap paper.

Established and well published writer Julian Preston offered some terrific professional writing advice and encouragement. It was he who unintentionally reminded me that it's a long time since I passed the English Language GCE O-Level.

Finally, a big thanks to Bill Cameron from Nairn, and Murcia in Spain, who has put a lot of effort into giving final drafts a thorough testing. It is only after his work that I feel confident enough to publish this book.

None of those people who helped me get this book into print must be held in anyway responsible for faults remaining in it. Those will be entirely all my own work!

Contents

Copyright   ii

Acknowledgements   iii

Introduction   1
    The Path to Cawdor   2
    Shakespeare's Macbeth - Summary 4

Where, When & Witches   7
    Moray, Forres   8
    A Desert Place   10
    Shakespeare & the Forres Witches 12
    Morayshire - Macbeth's Hillock   14

The True Macbeth & The Church   17
    Castles in Dingwall, Ross-shire 18
    Lineage, Status and Rank   20
    Castle Rait, Nairn   22
    The Black Isle & Fortrose Cathedral 24
    Norse Settlement, Power and The Church 26
    Durham and the Failed Scottish Adventures 28
    Elgin - The Bishopric of Moray   30
    Macbeth - the Pope & the Church 32

Palaces & Castles   37
    11th Century Castles   38
    Elgin Castle   40
    Bamburgh and Earl Siward   42
    Inverness Castle   44
    Thane of Glamis, or Cromarty?   46
    Torridon Fort - Burghead   48
    Cawdor Castle   50
    Brodie Castle   52
    Macduff's Castle   54

Battles, Death & Succession   57
    Sueno's Stone - Forres   58
    Pitgavney, Loch Spynie & Spynie Palace 60
    Dunsinane Hill - Perthshire   62
    Macbeth shall never vanquish'd be..... 63
    Lumphanan, Aberdeenshire   64
    Saint Finan's Cemetery, Lumphanan 66

Photographer's Notes   69
    The Camera   70
    Imaging Software   71
    Desk Top Publishing   71
    Finally   71

Introduction

The Path to Cawdor

It all started with this photograph. In 2009 my wife and I moved to a development known as Firhall Village in Nairn. The River Nairn runs beside Firhall, which was once the estate and mansion house owned by the Grants of Rothiemurchas. During our first winter I took frequent walks on the path by the river. The path runs several miles from Nairn Harbour to Cawdor Village. On one such walk I took this photograph. I called the shot The Path to Cawdor, hinting at a journey into the darkness, myth and history that was Macbeth, Thane of Cawdor.

I knew, of course, that neither the path, nor Cawdor had much to do with the real Macbeth. However, the popularity of the photograph with friends and relatives gave me the idea of combining two of my great interests, photography and history. I would compile a book of Macbeth connections which would include photographs of locations associated somehow with Macbeth. This would provide ample opportunity for taking interesting new photos and researching the history of the each location. The book would include favourite photos while associated text would discuss the Macbeth connection, history and location.

I started the collection by getting a copy of Shakespeare's play for reference and doing some on-line research. It soon became clear that the book would not be as straight forward as I had expected. I discovered that, not only was the portrayal of Macbeth by Shakespeare well wide of the mark, but that valid historical evidence about the real Macbeth is thin on the ground. Some accepted stories of the real man turned out to be unsubstantiated. For example, some in Dingwall, Ross-shire, believed that Macbeth was born in that place and lived in Dingwall Castle.

It was my attempts to verify this, through the University of the Highlands & Islands, that led me to Dr Fiona Watson, writer, historian and broadcaster. She advised me that there was no evidence that Macbeth was born or lived at Dingwall.

It is Fiona who has kept me straight about many historical matters, and has given much kind support on my journey. This is not intended to be a serious academic study with long lists of sources, publications and suchlike. I would like, though, to give Fiona a special thanks here for her support. I recommend to anyone wishing to learn more of the real Macbeth that they should read her book, "Macbeth - A True Story".

Interesting diversions and new stories cropped up to cause the content of this book to be broader than originally intended. In addition, my enjoyment of photographing castles, churches and cathedrals has led to the inclusion of some in this book with little connection to either the real or fictional Macbeth. I hope the reader will forgive and, hopefully, appreciate these tour diversions.

There is a lot of uncertainty and contradiction about 11th century Scottish history. This was frustrating and confusing, even when writing an informal book like this. At the same time, though, it was exciting trying to make sense of it all and just get a glimmer of understanding about life in those times. As a result I have thoroughly enjoyed learning about Macbeth and putting this book together. I sincerely hope that you the reader can enjoy taking The Path to Cawdor just half as much as I have.

Brian Lockey, August 2015

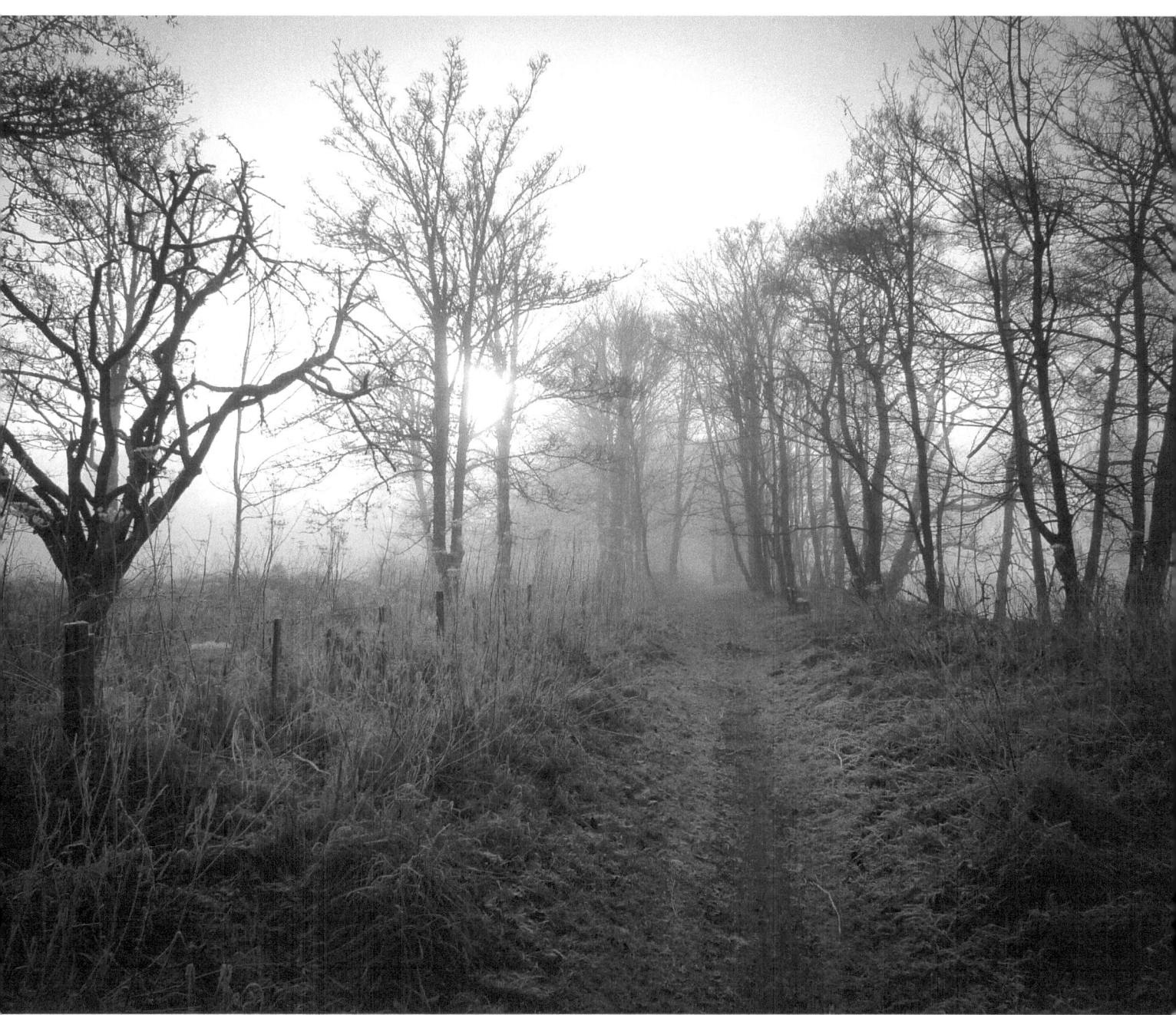

Shakespeare's Macbeth - Summary

Macbeth has led King Duncan's forces to victory against Norse forces and a treacherous Thane of Cawdor. He and companion Banquo are on their way to Forres. Three Witches meet nearby. They tell Macbeth that he will be "Thane of Cawdor!" and "king hereafter". Banquo learns that his descendants shall be kings. Both are suspicious but when Macbeth later hears he has been made the new Thane of Cawdor, he begins to wonder if he may be king as well. King Duncan then announces that his son, Malcolm will be the new Prince of Cumberland. Macbeth sees Malcolm as a threat to his destiny.

Lady Macbeth hears of the Witches' prophecies for her husband and plans King Duncan's murder while he stays at Macbeth's castle. Macbeth does not want to murder his King but Lady Macbeth prevails. Macbeth kills Duncan in his sleep. When news of Duncan's death spreads through the castle Macbeth, in false rage, blames and kills two drunken guards. King Duncan's sons, Malcolm and Donalbain both flee Macbeth's castle as a precaution. This leaves Macbeth free to be crowned the new King of Scotland. Macduff, Thane of Fife, snubs Macbeth's coronation at Scone to go to Fife instead.

Banquo wonders if Macbeth killed King Duncan to make the Witches' prophecy fact. Macbeth fears that the existence of Banquo's son could mean his dynasty will be short-lived. He arranges to discreetly kill both Banquo and his son. The murderers kill Banquo but his son Fleance escapes. Macbeth later arranges for Macduff's entire family to be murdered.

In the meantime Lady Macbeth's insanity becomes clear while dead King Duncan's son Malcolm and Macduff discuss how Scotland under Macbeth's rule has been plunged into despair. Nobleman Lennox and another Lord discuss affairs in the kingdom and mention that an army is being formed in England to fight Macbeth. The Three Witches now prophesy Macbeth's downfall, that he should "beware Macduff.." At the same time he is reassured that "none of women born....Shall harm Macbeth" and that he has nothing to fear until "Great Birnam wood" moves to "high Dunsinane hill".

Macbeth's enemies gather near his castle at Dunsinane. He prepares to fight while holding onto the prophecy that he will only be defeated when the nearby Birnam Wood moves on his castle. With his troops loyally around him, Malcolm orders each to cut down a branch from the nearby Birnam Wood and his army, now camouflaged, head towards the castle at Dunsinane.

Meanwhile as Macbeth coldly shrugs off the news of Lady Macbeths's death he learns that Malcolm's camouflaged forces are moving on his castle. He realizes what this means but fights on and is eventually confronted by Macduff. Macbeth says he is unable to be killed by a man, naturally born. Macduff tells him he was born by Caesarian section. Macbeth is killed and order is restored when Malcolm is hailed as the new King of Scotland.

In complete contrast to the darkness of Shakespeare's Macbeth here is a more peaceful modern scene. It is a photo' of Cawdor Castle in 2015.

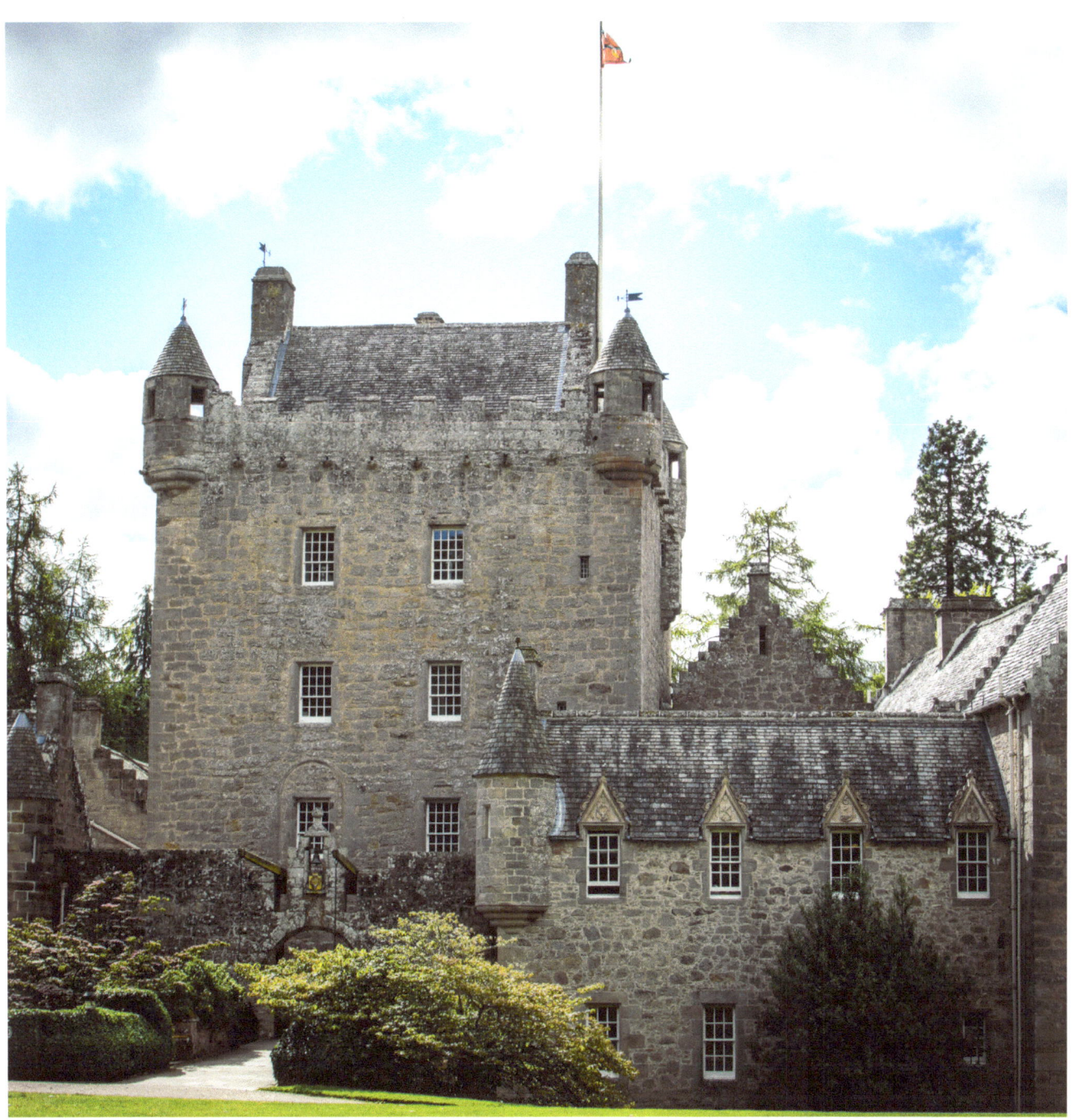

Where, When & Witches

Moray, Forres

Early Scottish History is complex and it is difficult to make sense of the twists and turns which brought about modern Scotland. Around the time of Macbeth the situation was particularly obscure. Norman Davies, in his book "Europe - A History", sums up the confusion in his chapter covering the period 750-1270;

> *"Whilst the English battled the Danes, the rest of the British Isles witnessed a long, complex struggle with Vikings and Celts. Fluctuating federations of Northmen fought fluctuating leagues of Celtic princes......In the north of Britain the Gaelic King of Kintyre, Kenneth MacAlpin (d.c860) was the first to join Picts with Scots, and thereby to launch the concept of a united 'Scotland'. After that, a three-sided contest emerged between the Gaels of the Highlands, the English of the lowlands, and the Norsemen of the outer isles."*

As if to prove the confusion within this quotation, it seems that MacAlpin is not now regarded by all historians as the first King of a unified Scotland.

England, also in a state of change at that time, was mainly governed by Northmen (or Norsemen, both broad terms covering peoples from Scandinavia) such as Canute. This England, according to one map of Canute's Kingdom, reached up the Eastern side of Britain and included Lothian and the modern Edinburgh area.

A later 12th century map shows the "Principality of the Cumbrians", including modern Glasgow, which sat between Alba (the Gaelic name for Scotland) and England.

So, the England referred to by Shakespeare in the play, could have included an area covered by modern Scotland. It would therefore be difficult to be certain of the ancestry of many of the characters, English and Scottish, mentioned in the play.

Forres, which features much in the play, is quite an ancient town. Robin Smith (The Making of Scotland, Canongate Books, 2001) suggests that Forres might be the Varis, indicated by Ptolemy in AD 140 when that

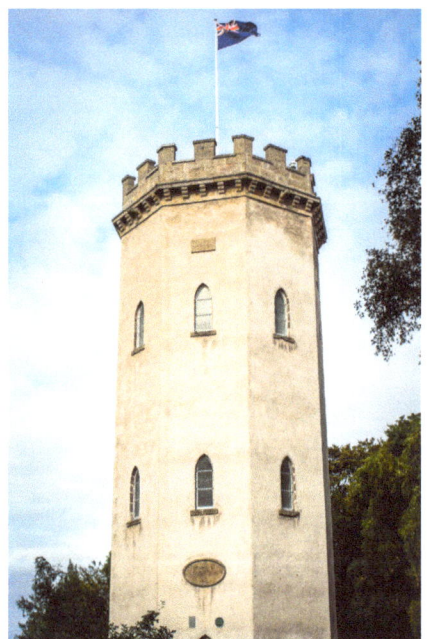

place was directly accessible from the sea. The area was subject to Viking raids and that is possibly why the early history of Forres and Moray is obscured.

This landmark tower was built as a memorial to Horatio Nelson in 1806. It is at the top of Cluny Hill in Forres and is the same hill on which Three Witches are said to have met their death.

The granite obelisk, opposite, was erected in 1857. It was erected to commemorate James Thompson, a surgeon who saved many lives in the Crimea. Of significance here is the fact that this monument is on the site where Forres Castle, as referred to by Shakespeare, once stood.

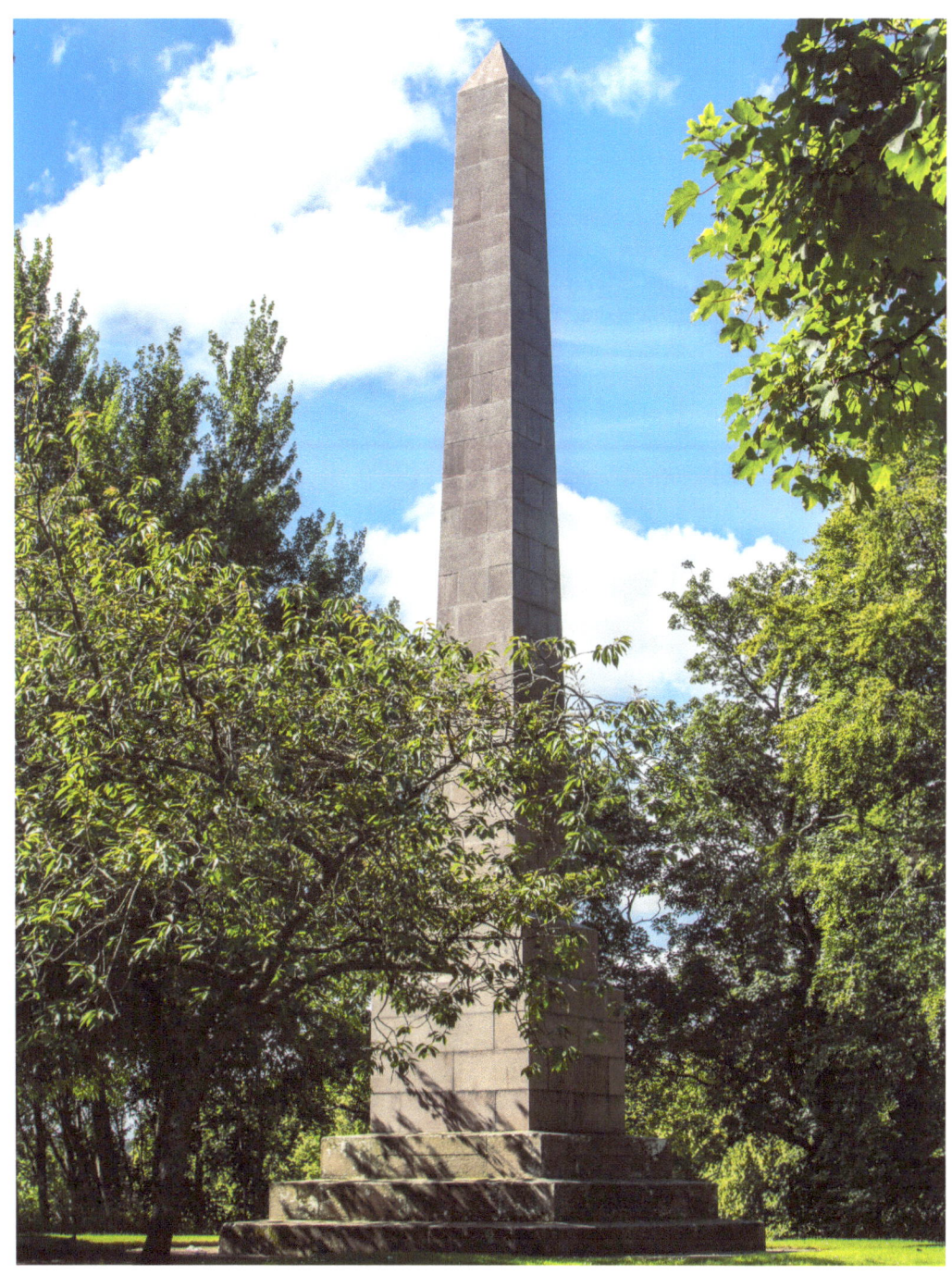

A Desert Place

Act 1 Scene 1 of the play opens with the three witches meeting at a desert place. English usage today might mislead many at this early stage in the play. Moray, and Forres in particular, couldn't be more unlike a desert. The lower ground, by the Moray Firth is, in fact, a very fertile area. This is what has made it a desirable place to pillage, conquer, rule and settle.

However, the scene directions actually refer to a deserted place somewhere near Forres. Even today it is not at all difficult to find such a place where witches could meet and several options are mentioned in this book. There are many quiet woods and forests in the area and, just a few miles further inland, the land rises to where there is a notable absence of trees and an increased presence of cold, wind and heather. It is reasonable to assume though, that canny witches would avoid the discomfort of wild mountain heaths and chose a hidden, quiet and dry area for their desert place.

This photograph is of a clearing near the edge of Dulsie Wood close to the village of Ferness, Nairnshire. While being about 11 miles from Forres, the site is typical of the area. With the foxgloves as stand-ins for witches, it could easily be the type of deserted place Shakespeare had in mind when he wrote the play.

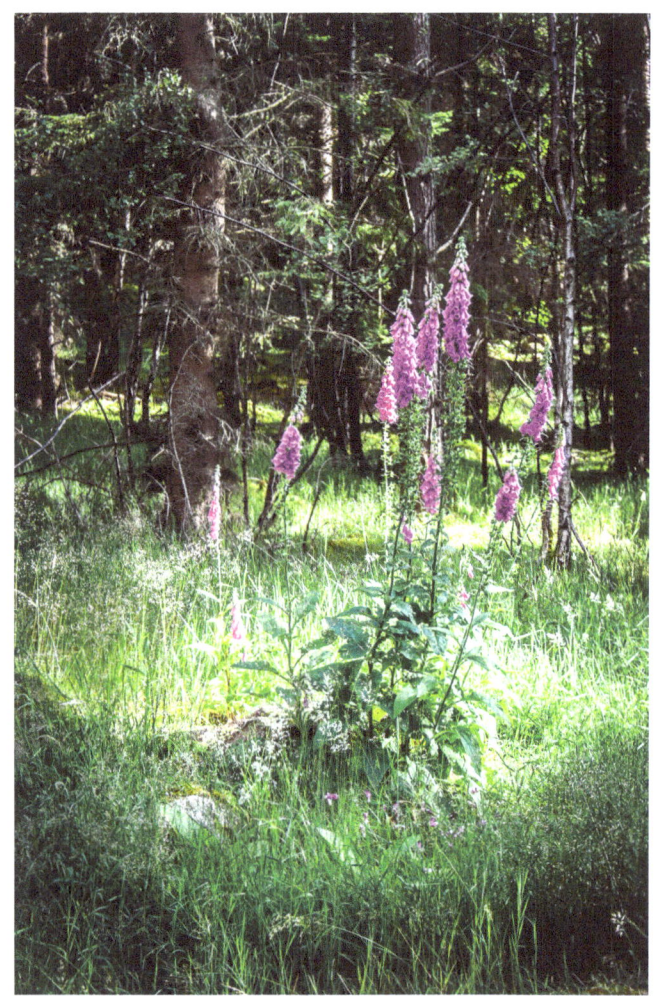

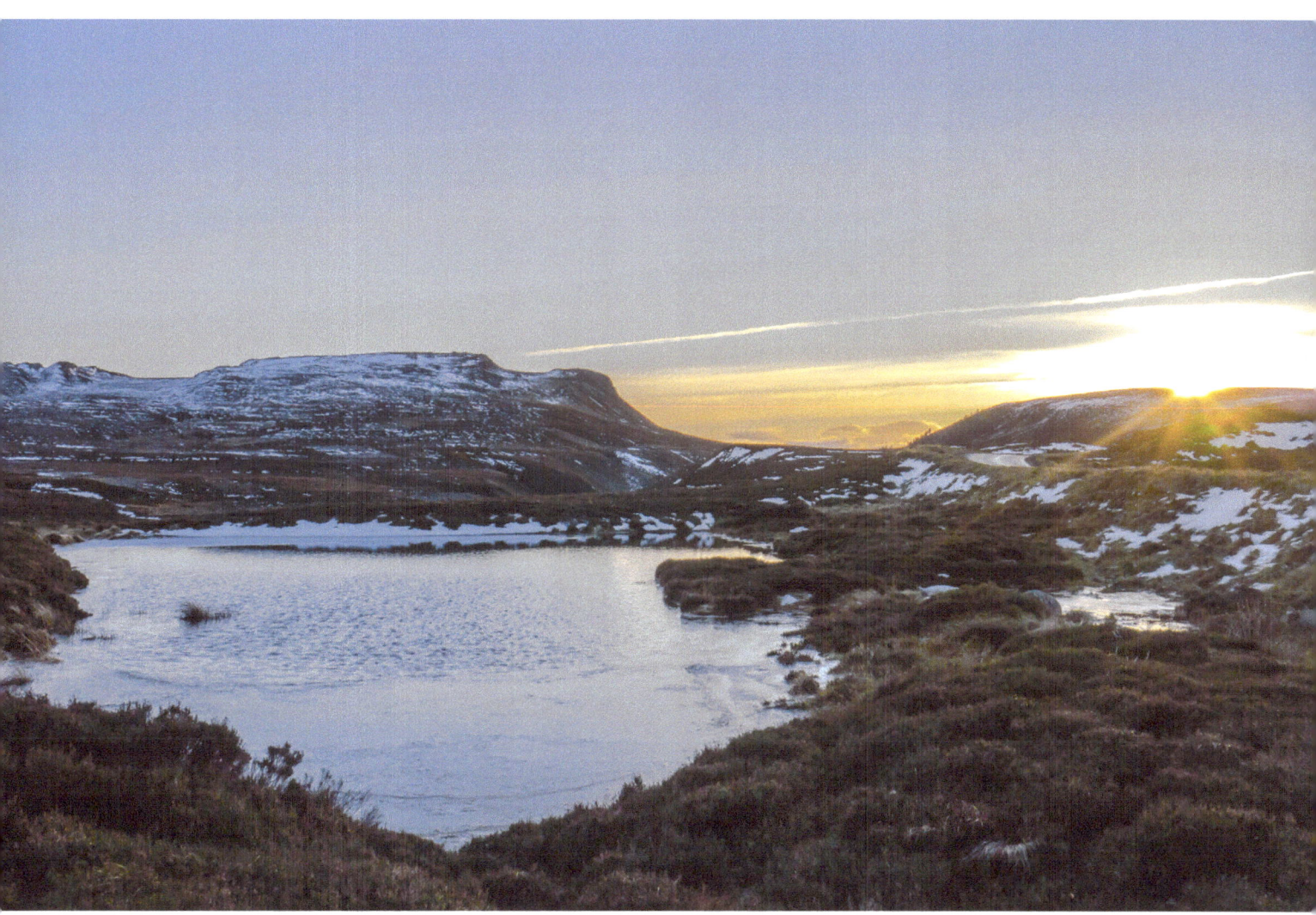

The south of Moray, where it is furthest away from the Firth, is quite unlike parts already mentioned. It is high, bleak and usually lots colder than the coastal lands. This is the kind of terrain where some Shakespeare experts believe that first crucial meeting between Macbeth and the witches took place. The photograph here was taken from the southern edge of modern Nairnshire not far north of the Cairngorms. The road, just visible on the right, is the B9007 which runs from near Forres, towards Carrbridge, the infamous A9 and Perth beyond.

Shakespeare & the Forres Witches

One might ask what witches have to do with the business of Kingship, real or fictional. Witches do not feature, at least with any known significance, in the life of the real Macbeth, so why in the play? According to Sir Roy Strong in "The Story of Britain", King James VI of Scotland was obsessed with witches. In fact James felt so strongly about the evil influence of such creatures that in 1597 he wrote and published a book about satan and witchcraft called 'Daemononlogie'. In the book he approves and supports witch-hunting.

Some believe that Shakespeare later wrote Macbeth largely to ingratiate himself with James, who had also become King James I of England in 1603. How better to achieve his aim than by making witches, and their evil ways, so significant to the play?

To add a little more relevance, if not reality, to the plot of Shakespeare's Macbeth, there is a local Moray legend about three witches. In AD 962 King Dubh (Duff), the son of Malcolm I, ascended the throne of Alba. During his reign he fell ill and was unable to govern with the firm hand so essential in those times. During his weakness a rebellion arose, as they were prone to do so in those days. The legend tells of Duff's solders, while seeking out rebels, coming across three old hags in the process of burning an effigy of the king on an open fire.

Each hag was arrested, forced into a barrel of hot oil and rolled down Cluny Hill at Forres. For good measure the barrels had spikes pushed through them. Accounts say the barrels were burnt at the foot of the hill and that three stones were placed where each barrel stopped. One stone remains today with an iron plaque describing its significance.

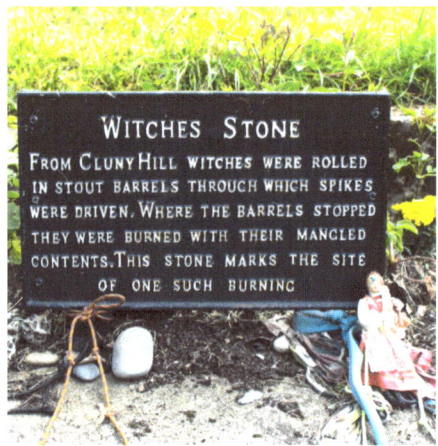

Curiously this stone is by the road just outside of Forres Police Station, as though intended to demonstrate that the meting out of justice has changed a tad since the 10th century.

It is said that King Duff started to make a full recovery from his illness immediately the witches were despatched. Early historians of Scotland were not as reliable as modern writers. Possibly this tale was accepted as fact, and believed by the likes of both Shakespeare and King James.

One wonders if modern day witches, or witch believers, regard the stone spot as shrine-like or having some spiritual significance. On different occasions in 2015 it has had; a dark sequined cloth draped over the plaque, a bunch of purple carnations resting there, two knotted scarves, a small stone with a hole in it and string tied through, another stone with what could be an eye scratched on it, a small doll and a collection of knotted laces!

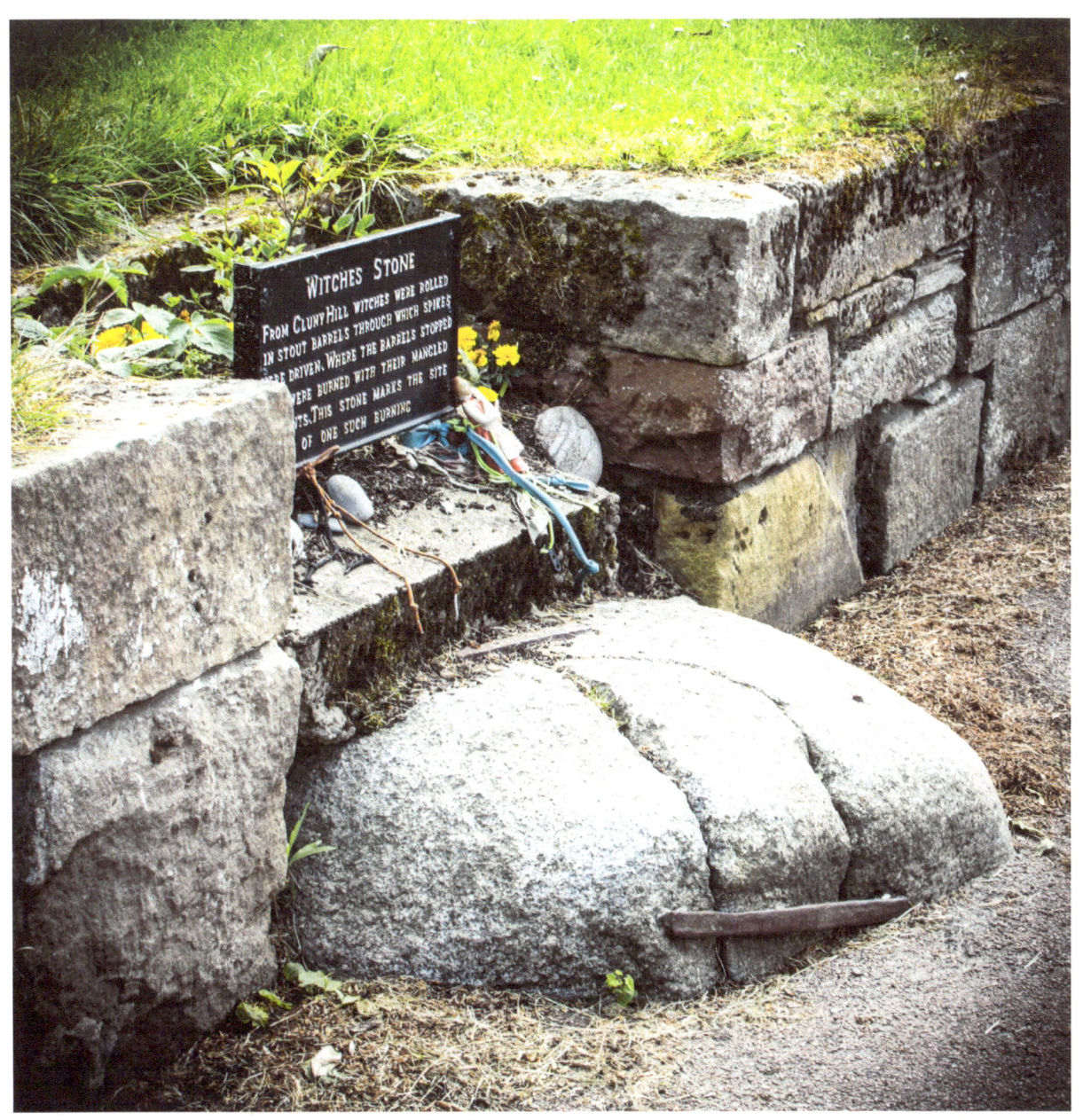

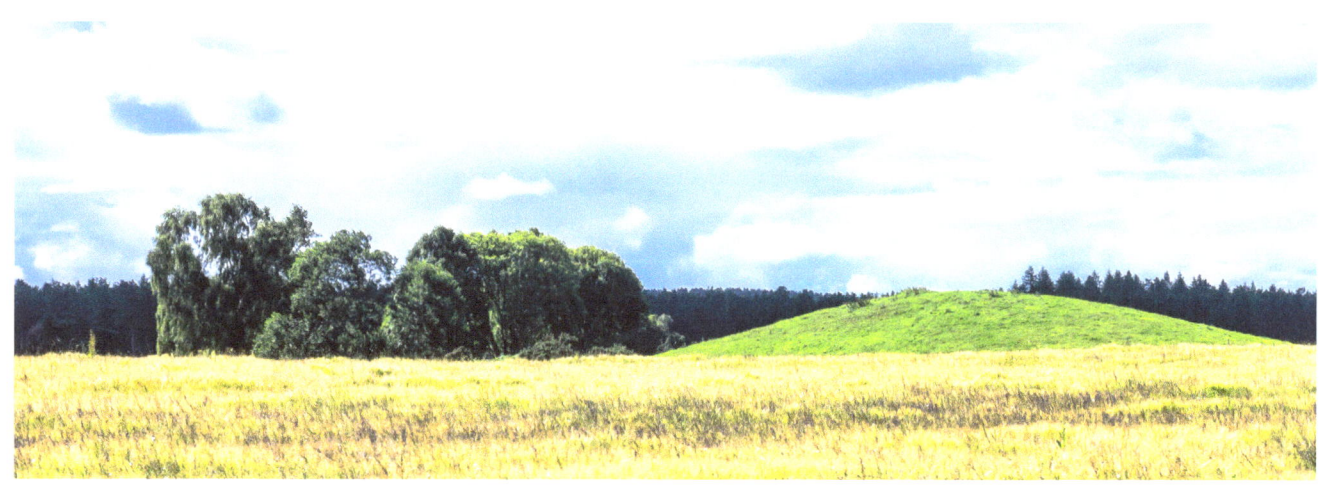

Morayshire - Macbeth's Hillock

There seems to be a compelling case for both Shakespeare's inclusion of witches, and the focusing of activity at Forres. The Forres area had been subject for many years to bloody fighting and changes of ruler. It also had a castle which was the home of ancient kings and, for good measure, it had a legend of witches interfering with the rule of one of those kings.

As shown in these photographs, the area also has what is known as Macbeth's Hillock. This modest bump in a field is marked on Ordnance Survey Maps. It is in Morayshire and is not far from Brodie Castle, between Forres and Nairn. It had a reputation for being the "desert place" mentioned by Shakespeare where Macbeth first met the three witches.

Scotland seems to have acquired several such places where the Shakespeare witches allegedly chose to meet. It is not clear how this hillock it earned that particular reputation. Nor is it clear whether it's a natural or a man-made feature.

Considering its closeness to the A96 Inverness-Aberdeen main road, it is hardly remote enough for witches today. However, the nearby woodland would have been much more extensive in Shakespeare's day. Perhaps the hillock was once hidden in a woodland clearing and more suitable for gatherings of witches?

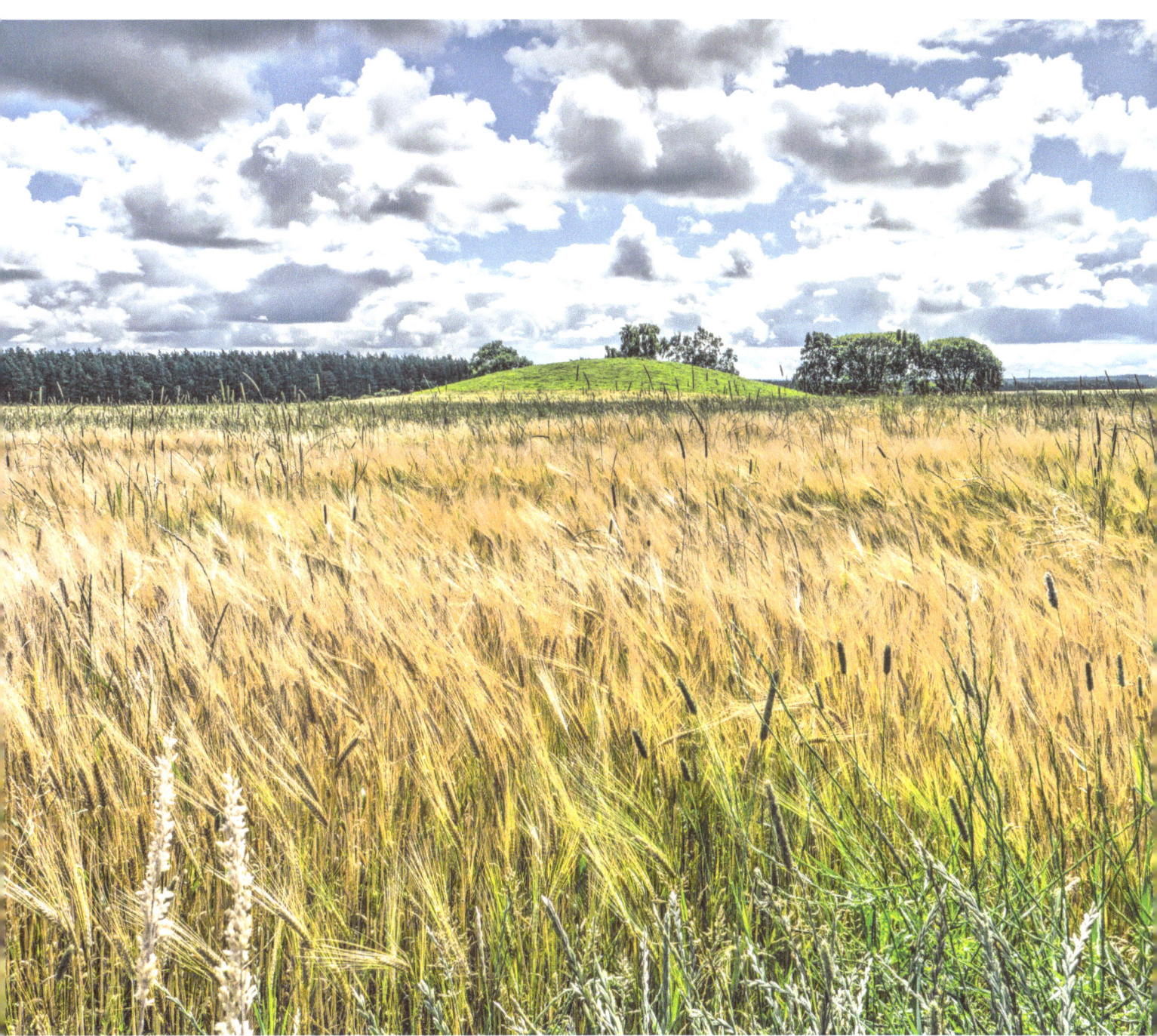

The True Macbeth & The Church

Castles in Dingwall, Ross-shire

It is not known exactly when or where Macbeth was born. Serious historians don't even know who his mother was. Others say that he was born in Dingwall around 1005 and that his mother was Donada, who was the second daughter of Malcolm II. Furthermore there are stories that, as a child, he lived in a Castle at Dingwall and played in the nearby River Peffery.

Dingwall, formerly the county town of Ross and Cromarty, lies near the head of the Cromarty Firth some 14 miles northwest of Inverness. In the early Middle Ages Dingwall was reputed to have the largest castle north of Stirling. Little is left of that castle today. On its site is the rather grand Castle House which was built in 1820. In the grounds is left a small fragment of a castle wall. Beside the nearby public road are the remnants of the old castle gatehouse, said to date to the 12th century. The photograph here shows the gatehouse as it actually is, i.e. slightly tilted.

Started in the 12th century Tulloch Castle, shown opposite, is about a mile from the site of Dingwall Castle. There is reputed to be an ancient tunnel which links the two castles. Tulloch Castle is now a pleasant, but allegedly, haunted hotel.

Documented history of Dingwall is vague or non-existent for the lifetime of Macbeth. It has been suggested, though, that the first Dingwall Castle was probably a Norse fortress. It is accepted that the Norse were the dominant force in that area from around the 9th century. The name Dingwall is derived from the Norse "thing", meaning a fixed meeting place. This was verified in 2013 when a mound (the thing) in Dingwall was excavated. A fragment of an iron vessel was found and the earth samples in the mound were carbon dated.

Archaeologists and historians now believe the mound was built, in the 11th century, on the instructions of Thorfinn "the Mighty". Thorfinn controlled Shetland, Orkney and the Northern Highlands. However, during Macbeth's lifetime he tried to extend his lands south, beyond the Cromarty Firth, on several occasions.

In this respect Shakespeare was largely correct in the first scene of the play where Scottish and Norse armies were almost routinely at war with each other.

Dingwall Castle, if it existed at the start of the 11th century, would therefore be a very unlikely home to a young Macbeth.

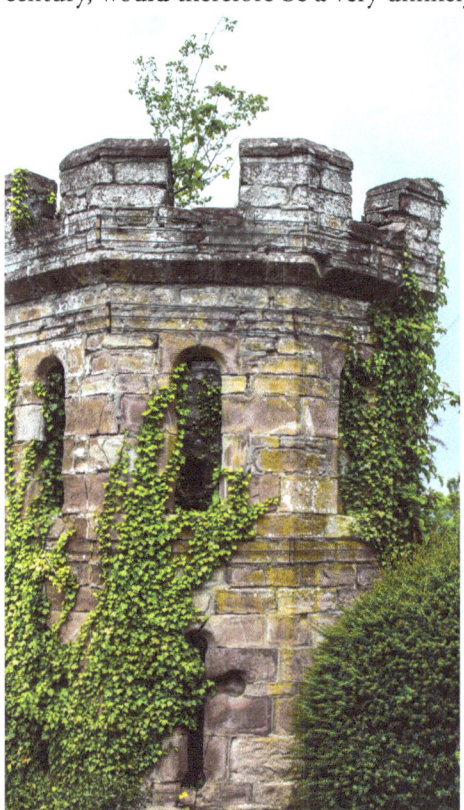

Scandinavian and Scottish races may have settled, farmed and lived together at the Southern edge of Thorfinn's domain. Nevertheless, it would have been for unsafe for anyone with Scottish royal blood to live anywhere north of Inverness.

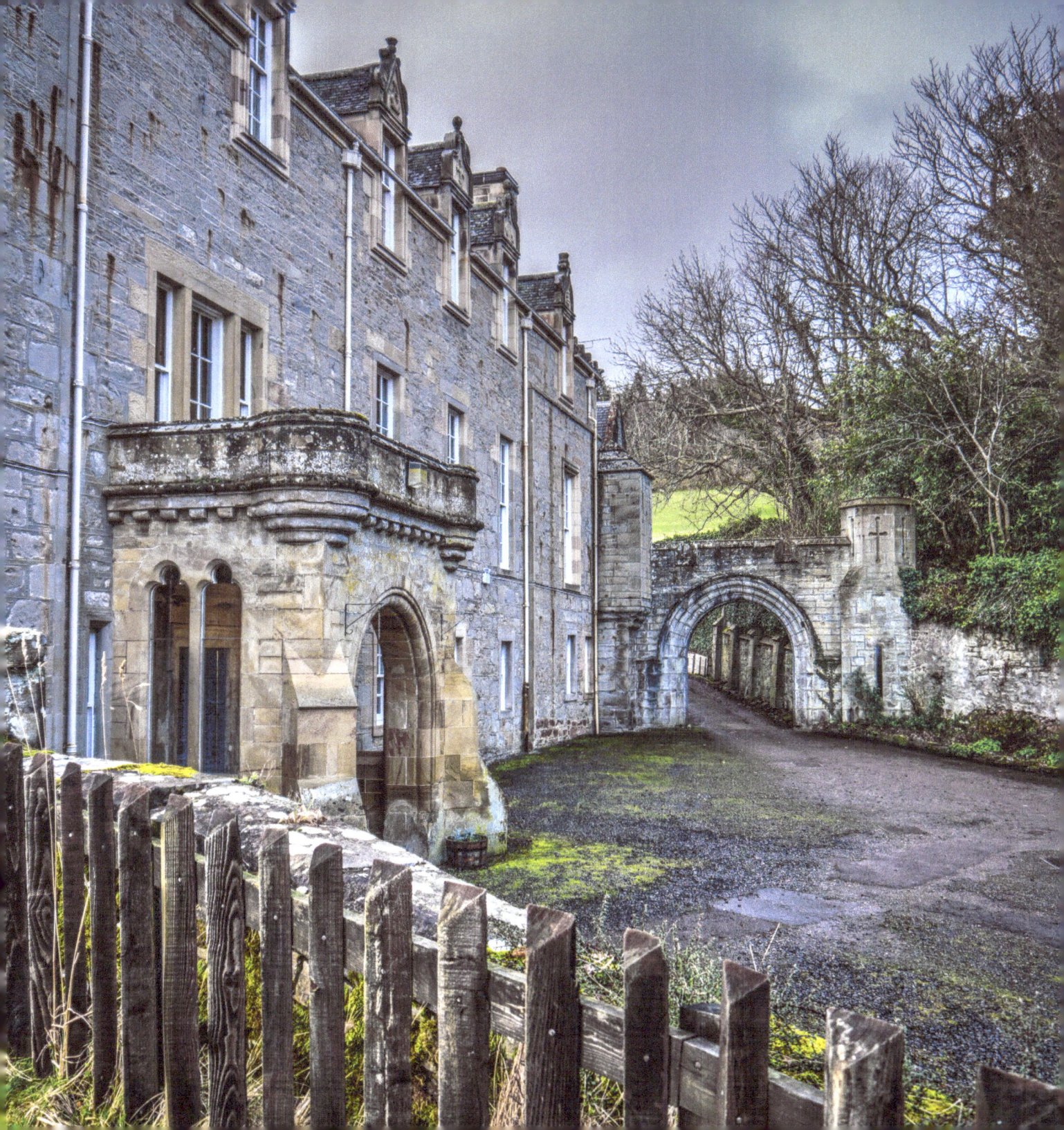

Lineage, Status and Rank

It is probable that Macbeth was born around AD 1000 somewhere in Moray. While it is not certain who his mother was, his father is known to be Finlay of Moray. Due to the almost unfathomable politics of the time, Moray was technically ruled by King Malcolm II of Scotland. At the same time, Finlay controlled Moray and probably resented rule by Malcolm in the south.

Furthermore, Finlay of Moray's mother, or grandmother, was "probably a daughter of either Indulf mac Constantine or Culen mac Indulf, kings from the line of Aed mac Kenneth" (Quoted from "Macbeth – A True Story" by Fiona Watson). This perhaps gave Finlay cause to believe he had enough of a blood connection to Kenneth mac Alpin, to claim a right to govern all Scotland.

Acquiring the post of King in those days seems to have been achieved by a combination of blood connection, strength of mind and body, political clout and often assassination of a relative. For the sake of simplicity, which Early Scottish History certainly does not exhibit, other influences on Scottish Kings and Kingdoms will therefore be bypassed. These include such complications as strong Irish-Gaelic connections, the existence of another Malcolm (of Moray), the ambitious Norse Orcadians and the Norse King of the English, Cnut.

The simplified scenario is that Finlay and Malcolm II kept a close eye on each other, each believing they had a right to the King of Scotland title. It follows that Macbeth would have similar ambitions.

Shakespeare's play is full of Thanes. In Act One, Macbeth is already Thane of Glamis then as a reward he is also made Thane of Cawdor. In fact the first real Thane of Cawdor was not appointed, by King Alexander II, until 1236. The rank of Thane does not seem to be used much in early medieval Scottish history and appears to be primarily an English term which was later applied to Scottish Earls or Lords.

A more appropriate title might have been that of Mormaer, which is a Gaelic name for a provincial ruler. In Irish Annals, the differences between terms Mormaer and King are indistinct. It is they that record that Finlay, the real Macbeth's father, was Mormaer/King of Moray. After a couple of royal family assassinations Macbeth inherited that ranking.

In onomatopoeic terms the word Thane conjures up images of a powerful, ruthless warrior-ruler. This alone would be good reason for Shakespeare to use that rank. The more appropriate title for the time, Macbeth, Mormaer of Moray, just does not have the same impact somehow. However, Shakespeare did work from earlier histories which may have retrospectively applied the term of Thane.

The current 7th Earl of Cawdor, of Clan Campbell of Cawdor, is the 26th Thane of Cawdor. The castle, shown here from the magnificent gardens, is not his home though. Angelika, the Dowager Countess Cawdor, "went to court to evict her stepson from his ancestral castle home." (from The Telegraph, 2002). It seems that Scottish family disputes are not all consigned to medieval history.

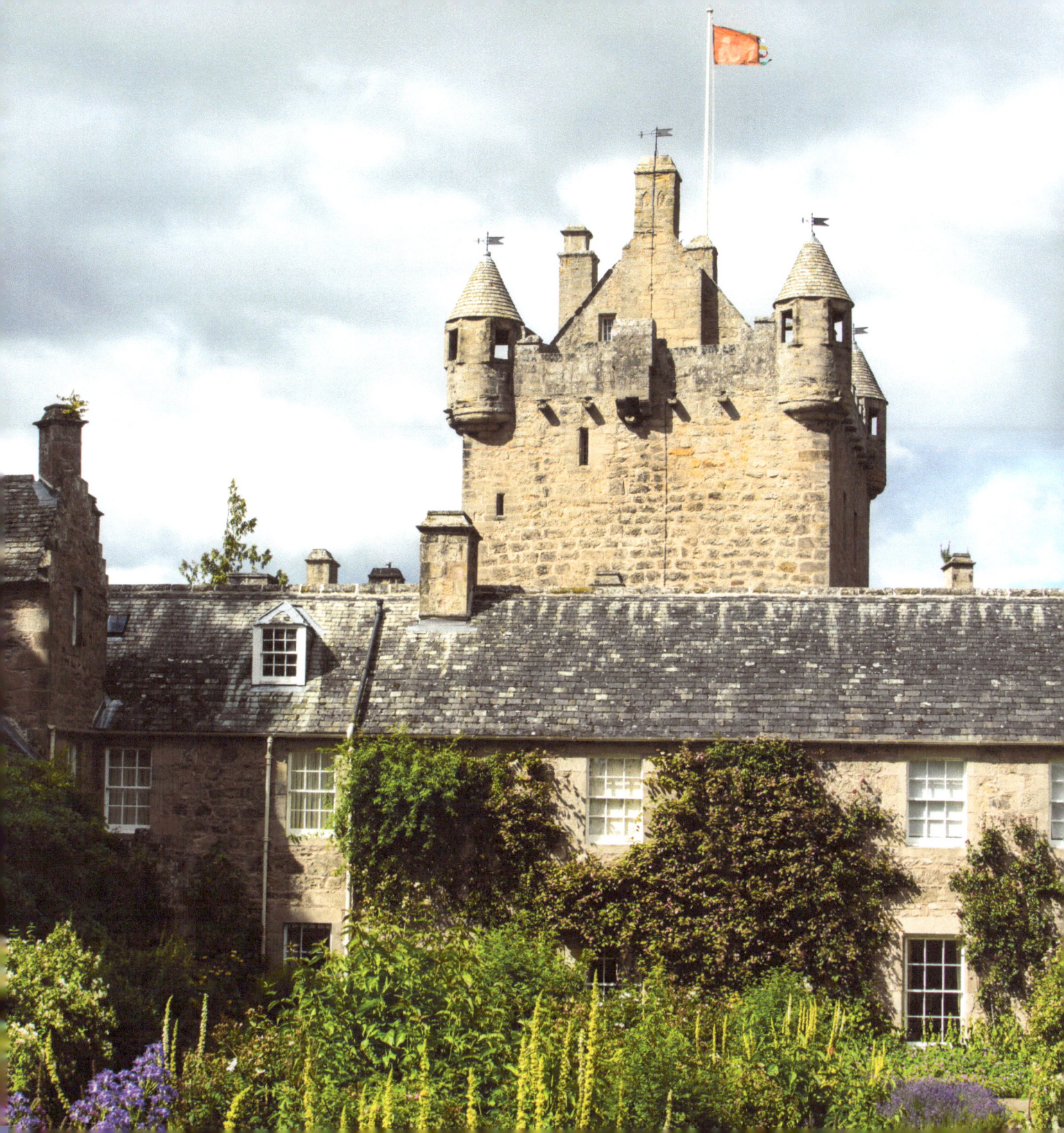

Castle Rait, Nairn

It was customary in 11th century high society to let sons, as potential heirs, to be breast-fed by a wet-nurse then sent away to be fostered by surrogate parents who would prepare the child for great things, perhaps Kingship. It is not known where Macbeth was actually brought up. He may well have been placed with a Gael family safely south of the Moray Firth, or maybe to the West, down the Great Glen, towards the West Coast. He may even have been brought up with relatives in Ireland. It is unlikely, though not impossible that he was born and spent his early years in ancient Moray at Caisteil Finlaih near Nairn. Little is known about this building, though its name indicates a probability that it belonged to Finlay (a.k.a. Findlay) of Moray. Finlay's Castle is shown on the Ordnance Survey maps and is known to be old enough and defensible enough to serve his purpose in troubled times.

Getting near to the castle site today using an OS map is difficult because of modern building, lack of public paths, lack of signage and many "private" fences in the area.

Following directions of a local businessman and along a vague path up into a wooded area leads to a clearing among the dead heather and gorse. At the far edge of the clearing is a small pile of large stones. Whether this is the remains of the Castle or not is difficult to say. However, it is close to the where the OS map had showed the Castle, and the site does have a commanding view of Nairnshire below.

Within about one mile of the Finlay Castle, in an area once called the Thanedom of Rait. is a later and more substantial ruin with a better known history. Being more photogenic than a pile of stones, it is shown on the opposite page. It is known as Rait Castle and, like Finlay Castle, it occupies higher ground above the more arable lower land which stretches to the Moray Firth.

It is believed to be the last 13th century hall castle left standing in Scotland. Stories are told of a grisly past alleged to be the reason the ruins have not been plundered for building stones. Such plundering appears to have been common and it may therefore be possible that stones from the ruins of Finlay Castle were used in the walls of the later Rait Castle.

There was, apparently, a local clan dispute. The chief of Clan Cumming (a.k.a. Comyn) invited rival Clan MacKintosh to a banquest at his Rait fortress. He planned to see off his rivals during the feast but didn't foresee the betrayal of his plan by his daughter who loved a young MacKintosh. The Chief survived the inevitable slaughter of his own Clan and afterwards pursued his daughter to a turret. He then sliced off her hands as she held on to a window ledge trying to escape him. She fell to her death. A young woman with no hands is said to haunt the castle since that bloody night in 1442. While there is some doubt about detail of the massacre of the Comyns, one has to wonder why no-one plundered the stones of the building when it was left empty.

Rait Castle is now part of the Cawdor Estate. There must have been some changes of local land-ownership over the centuries, since the 4th Thane of Cawdor was allegedly murdered by Sir Alexander Rait in 1405.

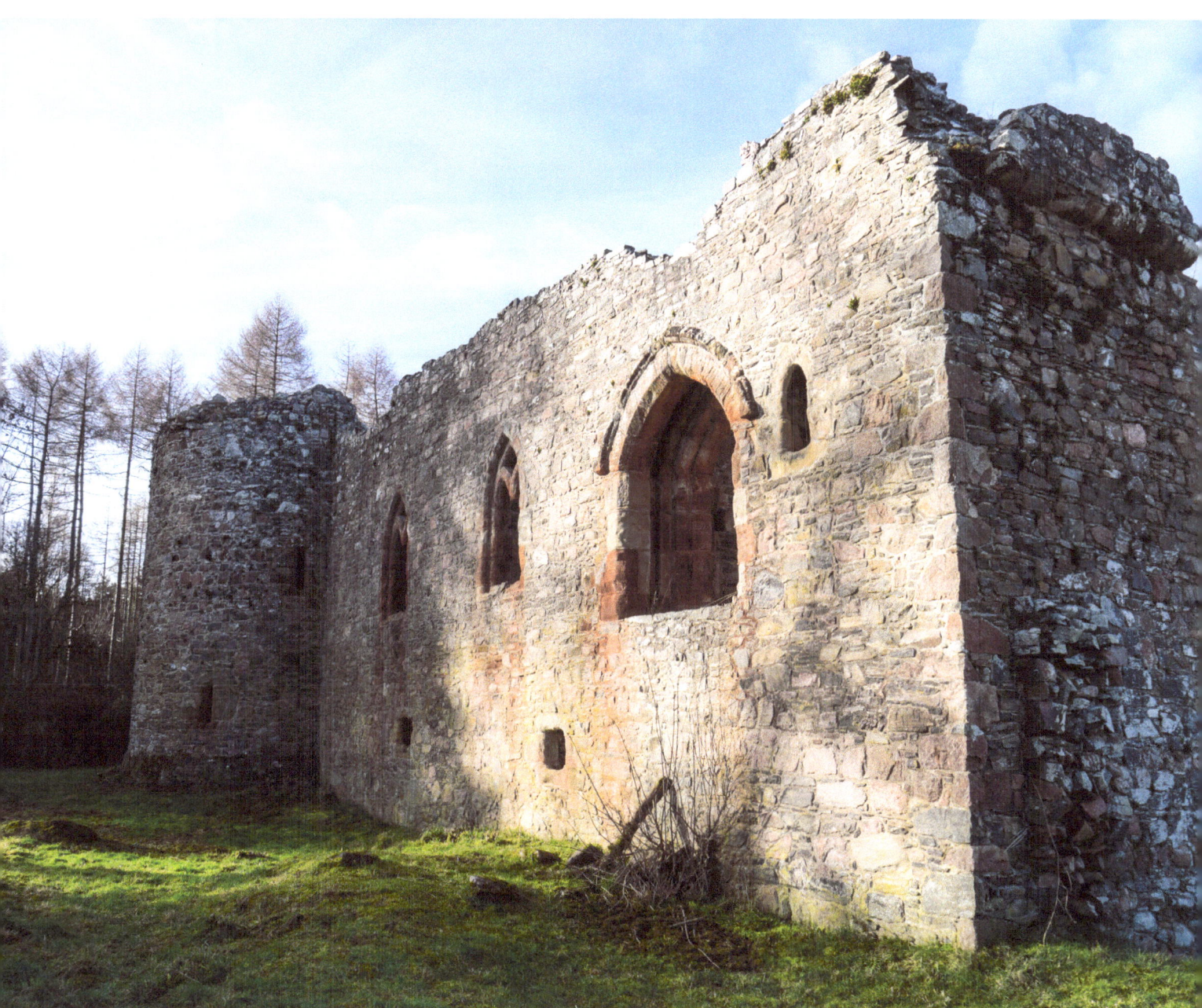

23

The Black Isle &
Fortrose Cathedral

Despite his ambitions, Finlay was not one of Moray's best strategists. It was under his leadership, perhaps with grown son Macbeth assisting, that Finlay once challenged Norse supremacy in Caithness, and lost. At the time Caithness was part of mainland Norse territory north of the Moray Firth.

This territory would have included Rosemarkie, on the Black Isle, for some of the time at least. Saint Moluag, a contemporary of St.Columba, is believed to have first established a church in Rosemarkie in the late 6th century. He is said to have evangelized the Picts of Scotland. He died in Rosemarkie, which became the site of an early Christian centre in the 8th and 9th centuries.

According to the Historic Scotland website, in 1236 Pope Gregory IX gave Bishop Robert permission to reform and enlarge the cathedral chapter. The website suggests that the permission prompted the move to a new cathedral at Fortrose dedicated to St Peter and St Boniface. These photos are of that Cathedral, which another internet source says was established in 1125.

The two sources therefore contradict each other regarding the time of establishment of the cathedral. As if to further illustrate how confusing much historical information is about medieval Scotland, the Historic Scotland website says that; "Tradition holds that the diocese of Ross existed as early as AD 700, and that it stood at Rosemarkie, a short distance north-east of Fortrose. The first recorded bishop, from around 1130, was Macbeth." Macbeth is derived from Gaelic, and means "Son of Life". It was a good, if common, Christian name of those times and quite suitable for a bishop, or a king.

For some time it might have been possible that Fortrose and Rosemarkie on the Black Isle were actually part of the Moray Mormaerdom. Ross and Moray are very close to each other in that area where the Moray Firth is very narrow. Perhaps Norsemen did not have all their own way in those parts easily reached by Finlay and his son?

However, Macbeth, son of Finlay, would be long dead at the time of the first Bishop of the Ross diocese, who was most likely to be a different "Son of Life".

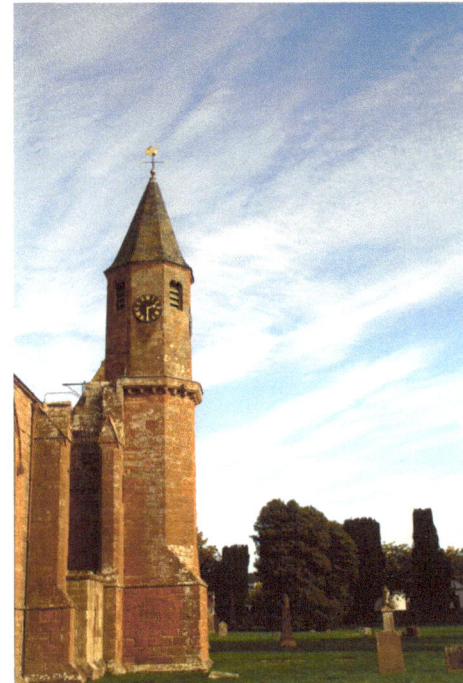

Despite questions raised regarding historical accuracy, it is clear that while Earthly rule and dominance is confusing, the church was widespread and powerful in this area.

It is also very illuminating to find that, far from believing in devil-worshipping witches, the continually feuding peoples and nations within Northern Scotland should share common religious beliefs.

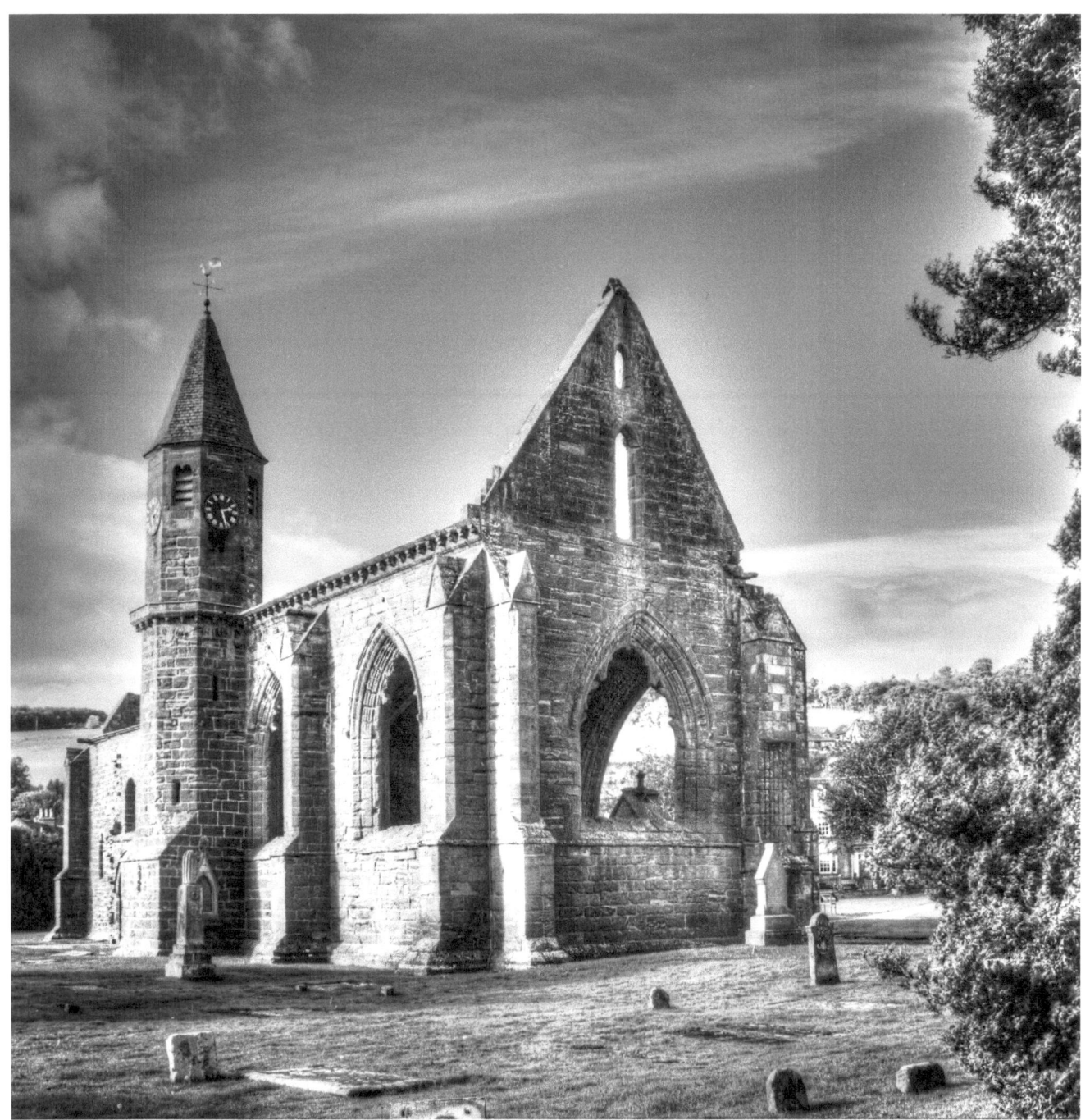

Norse Settlement, Power and The Church

The size, raw beauty, diversity and history of Norse controlled Scotland is truly fascinating. Sutherland and Caithness at the North and Western edges of mainland Scotland with the land, inlets and coastline around must have felt like home to the first raiders and settlers from Scandinavia.

Vikings made the Orkney Islands, north of Caithness, their home base for raiding expeditions against Norway as well as the coasts and isles around Scotland. Eventually, presumably after much settlement, farming and local fraternizing, Harold Hårfagre ("Fair Hair") annexed both Orkney and Shetland to Norway in AD 875. This did not put a stop, however, to the traditional summer pastime of raiding and land acquisition. They were a constant nuisance to Scots, Irish and English for a couple of centuries more. Indeed they feature in the opening Act of Shakespeare's play with Macbeth and Banquo returning after doing battle with them.

The surprising thing is that they were not all the wild heathen murderous raiders that fiction tends to portray. They were also docile settlers and farmers who keenly converted to Christianity. It appears that their first contacts with Christianity were through the native peoples and clerics they met in the British Isles and Normandy. The belief in one God was taken back to their homelands and, by the 12th century, Christianity was well established in Denmark, Norway and Sweden.

The extent to which the Norse became thoroughly Christian can be seen here in the magnificent cathedral of Saint Magnus that was started in 1137 at Kirkwall on Orkney.

The Bishop's Palace, see below, was built at the same time. It housed the cathedral's first bishop, William the Old. William took his authority from the Archbishop of Nidaros, now known as Trondheim, in Norway.

That much of North Britain, for centuries before and after Macbeth, was Norse governed is something easily forgotten today. Road signs to long established Norse settlements such as Wick, Thurso and Tongue currently translated into Gaelic seems disrespectful somehow.

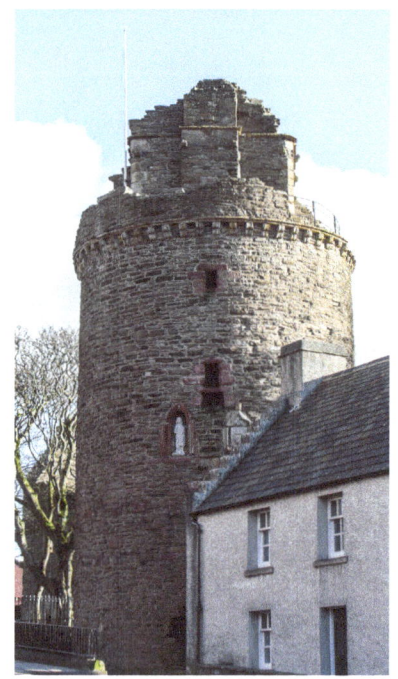

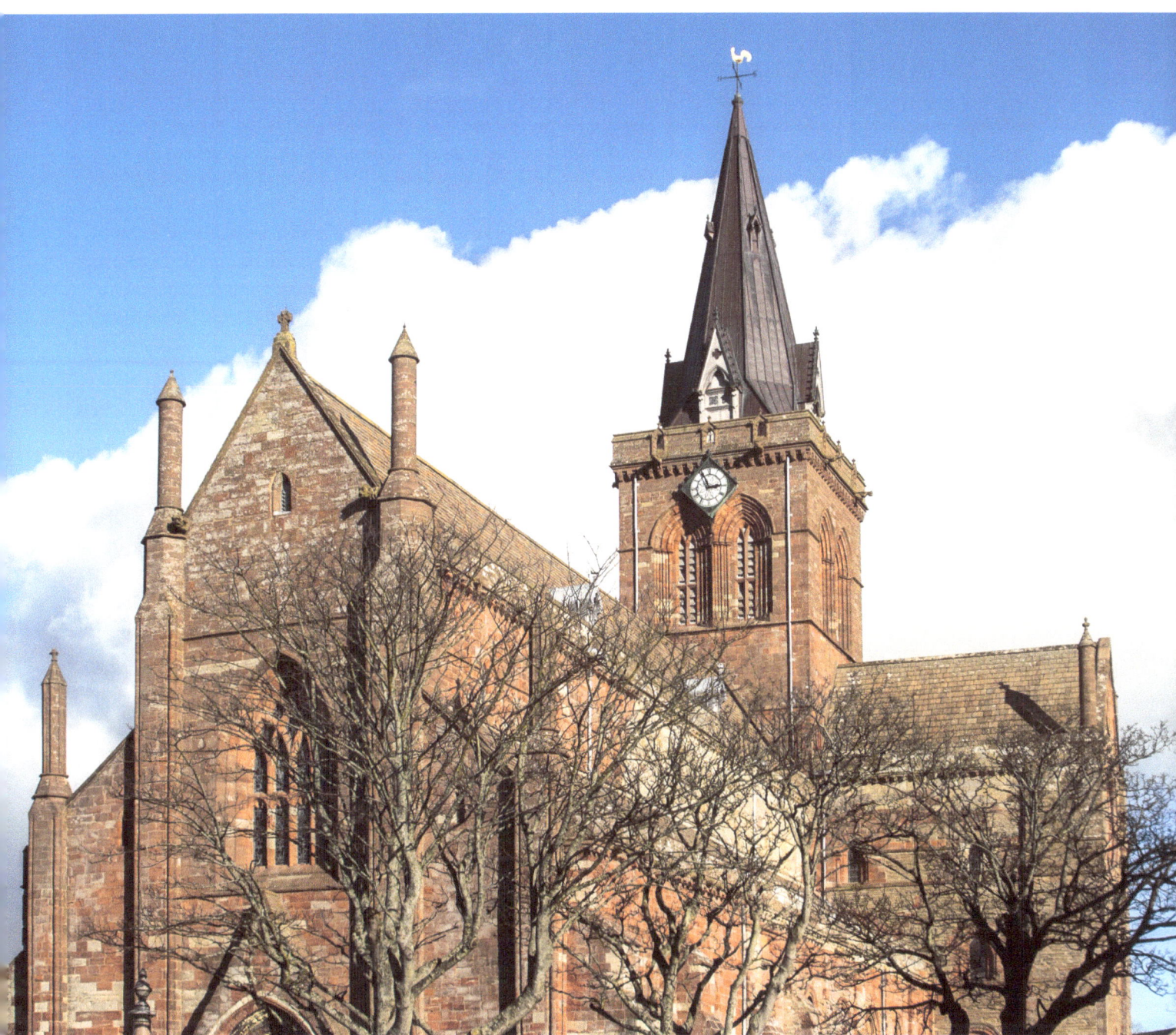

Durham and the Failed Scottish Adventures

Being 300 miles by modern road from Moray to Durham it is initially difficult to imagine how that city could have any association with Macbeth. There are, though, two such links and they are both reasonably well recorded. As one might expect from such turbulent times, both are related to power struggles.

In 1006, while Macbeth's father Finlay had designs on the Scottish crown, King Malcolm II was busy trying to establish his authority over ex-Northumbrian Lothian. He thought he could achieve this, and gain more territory, by fighting and pillaging across the modern day border and into the lands of the Bishops of Durham. Understandably Uhred of Northumbria took offence at this intrusion, massed a large force and thoroughly defeated and decimated Malcolm's army at Durham. It was after this event that Finlay might have thought his time had come and that it would be a good time to extend his own influence beyond Moray. As with his Northern adventures with Macbeth against the Norse into Caithness, Finlay's hopes and plans came to nothing. He did, however, consolidate his position in and around Moray, to the extent that on his death, Irish annals referred to him as a King to Scotland. Malcolm II, despite his failure at Durham, hung onto power and remained the true King of Scotland; probably with Moray technically being a part of his Kingdom, but beyond his real authority.

In 1040, Malcolm's grandson, King Duncan judged the time was right to have another try at invading Northumbria. Another confrontation occurred at Durham where his army was routed by whatever forces that city could muster on its own. This defeat was even more embarrassing than Malcolm's because no forces from the Earl of Northumbria were necessary. At this time Macbeth seems to have been Mormaer of Moray and had likely inherited his father's designs. It appears that Duncan knew well of the Macbeth threat to his own position. On return from the routing at Durham, it seems that Duncan chose to take his army and do battle with Macbeth and his Moray forces. It is not clear why he did this. It may have been because he did not want to appear a total failure after Durham, and that his reputation might be restored if he sorted out the Macbeth nuisance. What is clear, though, is that it was he who was the aggressor, and it was he who sailed with the royal army north to Moray. This is the same Duncan that Shakespeare has his fictitious Macbeth murdering with a dagger.

The magnificent Durham Cathedral shown here was started in 1093 to house a community of Benedictine monks and their shrine of St Cuthbert. They had been forced to move from Lindisfarne due to frequent raids by Vikings. It is not clear where these particular Vikings came from, or whether they were associated with Norse families resident in Northumbria at the time.

There is a castle just by the cathedral which shares the same hill and protective loop of the River Wear below. It was built in 1072 on the orders of William the Conqueror. The World Heritage Website says that "archaeological evidence suggests that an Anglo-Saxon defensive structure predated the Norman Castle". This Anglo-Saxon structure must surely have been the focus of the attacks by Kings Malcolm II and Duncan of Scotland.

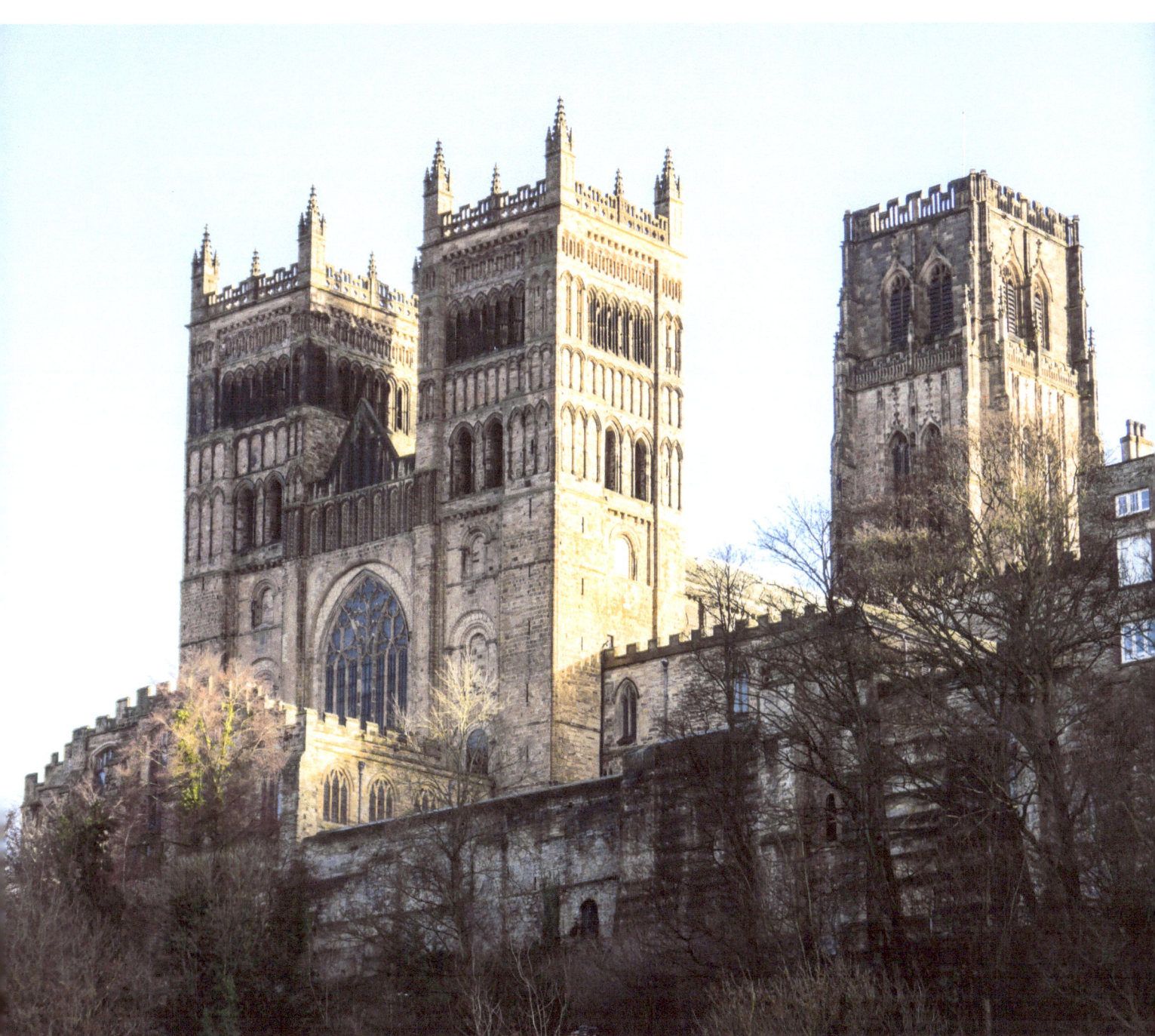

Elgin - The Bishopric of Moray

The Elgin area has long been the ecclesiastical centre of Moray and The Bishopric of Moray was established in the late 12th century. Until the 13th century, though, the "cathedral" rotated between Kinneddar, Birnie and Spynie churches. Early Bishops stayed at these places until they moved to Elgin itself. Building of the Elgin Cathedral (opposite) was started around 1224.

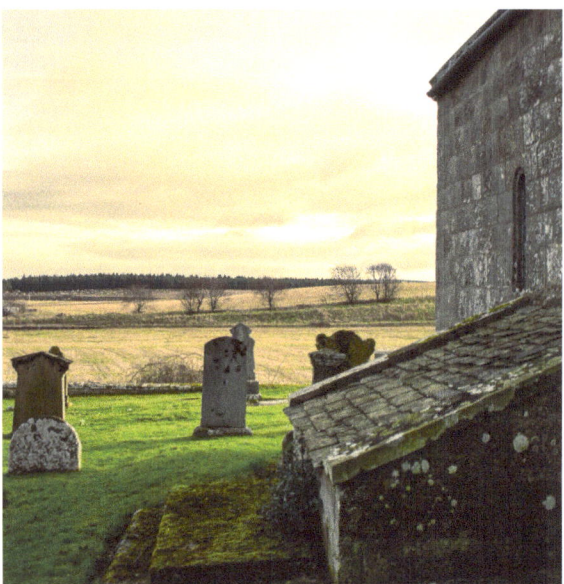

The Birnie Church, three miles south of Elgin and seen on this page, is one of very few Norman Churches in Scotland still in use for worship. It was built around 1140 but it had been an important site for worship much earlier. An ancient baptismal font in the church is thought to pre-date the building itself.

It is estimated that the first Celtic church at Birnie dated back to the 6th century. It was dedicated to St Brendan the Navigator, an Irish Saint.

The home of the Moray church has a non-spiritual connection with the real Macbeth story. When Duncan returned defeated after his failed adventure in Durham, he chose to do battle with Macbeth's forces. The battle site, just outside Elgin, is said to be Pitgavney. Some tales would have it that Macbeth killed Duncan in the battle. Others say that Duncan's bones were buried at Elgin Cathedral. One account adds that the battle was within sight of Elgin Cathedral.

The Elgin Cathedral connection with Macbeth is doubtful because it was built nearly two centuries after the Pitgaveny battle. Perhaps, though, a later historian, with an understanding of the geography, was really saying that the later-built structure could now be seen from where the fighting took place. This seems to fit with a probable battle site at the foot of a hill on which ruins of Spynie Palace currently sit. This is very near a few homes and a farm known now as Pitgavney. In Macbeth's day, Duncan's army would have reached that place via the open sea, the Moray Firth and Loch Spynie.

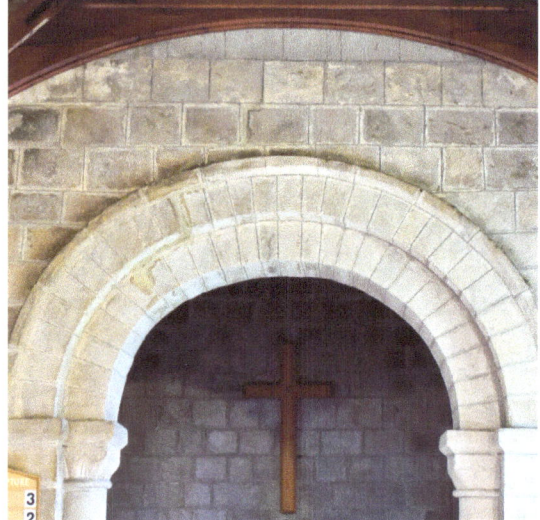

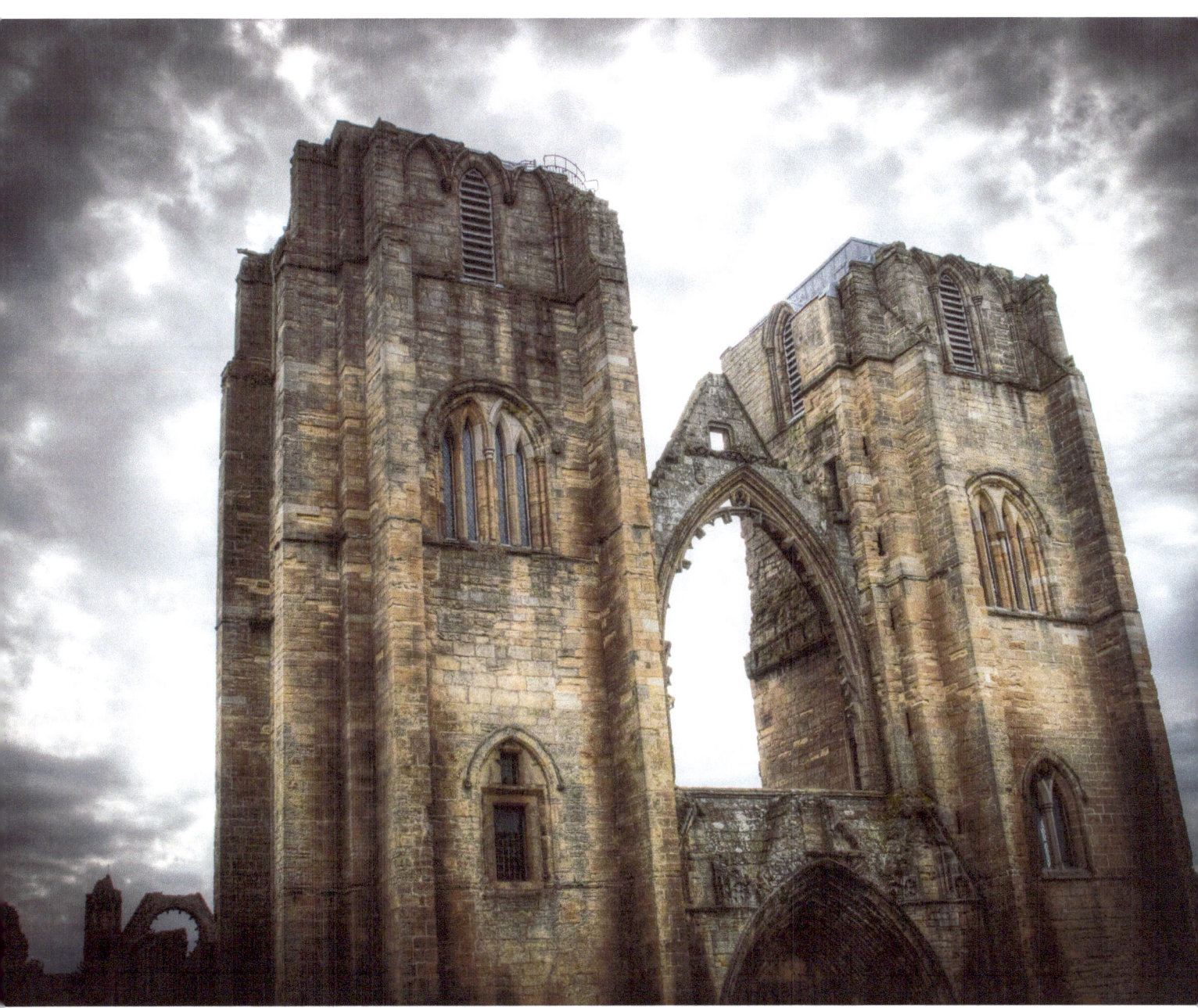

Macbeth - the Pope & the Church

One frequently reads in history about religious figures and how many had great influence, wealth and power. However, it takes a little more understanding, time and thought to fully appreciate that religion played such an enormous part in the lives of most people. We currently live in a largely materialistic and faithless society which tends to regard religion as an unnecessary restriction on lifestyle. A millennium ago things were much different. With a little insight one will realise that Shakespeare's inclusion in the Macbeth play of witches, and the exclusion of the religion, portrays a quite distorted impression of life in the 11th century. Perhaps the balance can be partially redressed here and religious belief given the historical relevance it deserves.

Following the work of missionary Columba in Inverness in the 6th century, the Nairn valley was evangelized and settled with churches. It is therefore quite clear that, after five centuries of Christianity, places of worship were commonplace in Macbeth's Moray.

Settlements having churches often took the prefix "Kil", being Celt for church. One such place by the River Nairn is Kilravock, where one such ancient church is said to have been sited.

The photo on this page is of Kilravock Castle, the tower of which was built later in 1460, shortly after completion of Cawdor Castle, three miles away. It is believed that both places were built by the same mason.

The main photo is of Kinloss Abbey. Also in Moray, Kinloss adjoins modern day Forres and is most definitely in Macbeth country. The Abbey was founded in 1150 by King David 1 and was first occupied by monks from Melrose Abbey. The Cistercians of Melrose themselves came from Rievaulx Abbey in Yorkshire. It is fascinating to see that, while Kings and would-be Kings were forever squabbling over territory, factions of the Church were similarly struggling over minds and hearts of the people. In Scotland most of the Church's influence came from Ireland with Columba. Yet later in the 12th century the Cistercians moved North to Moray from England, perhaps with a different take on Christianity.

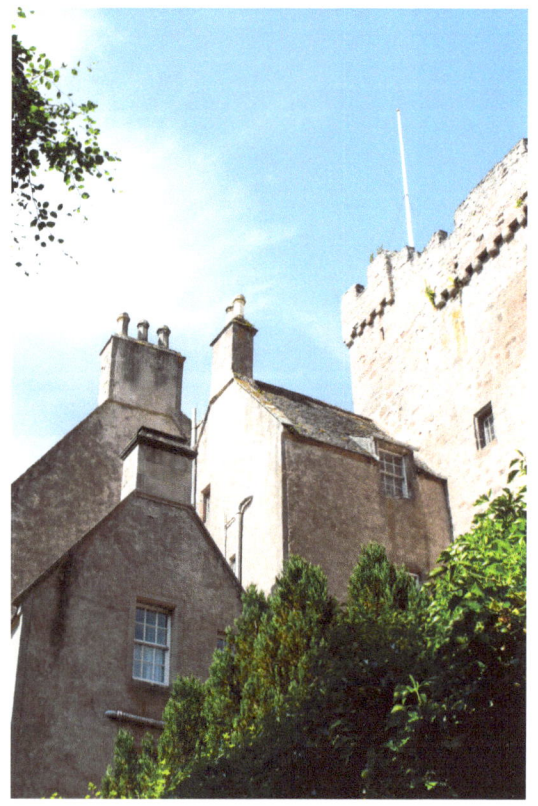

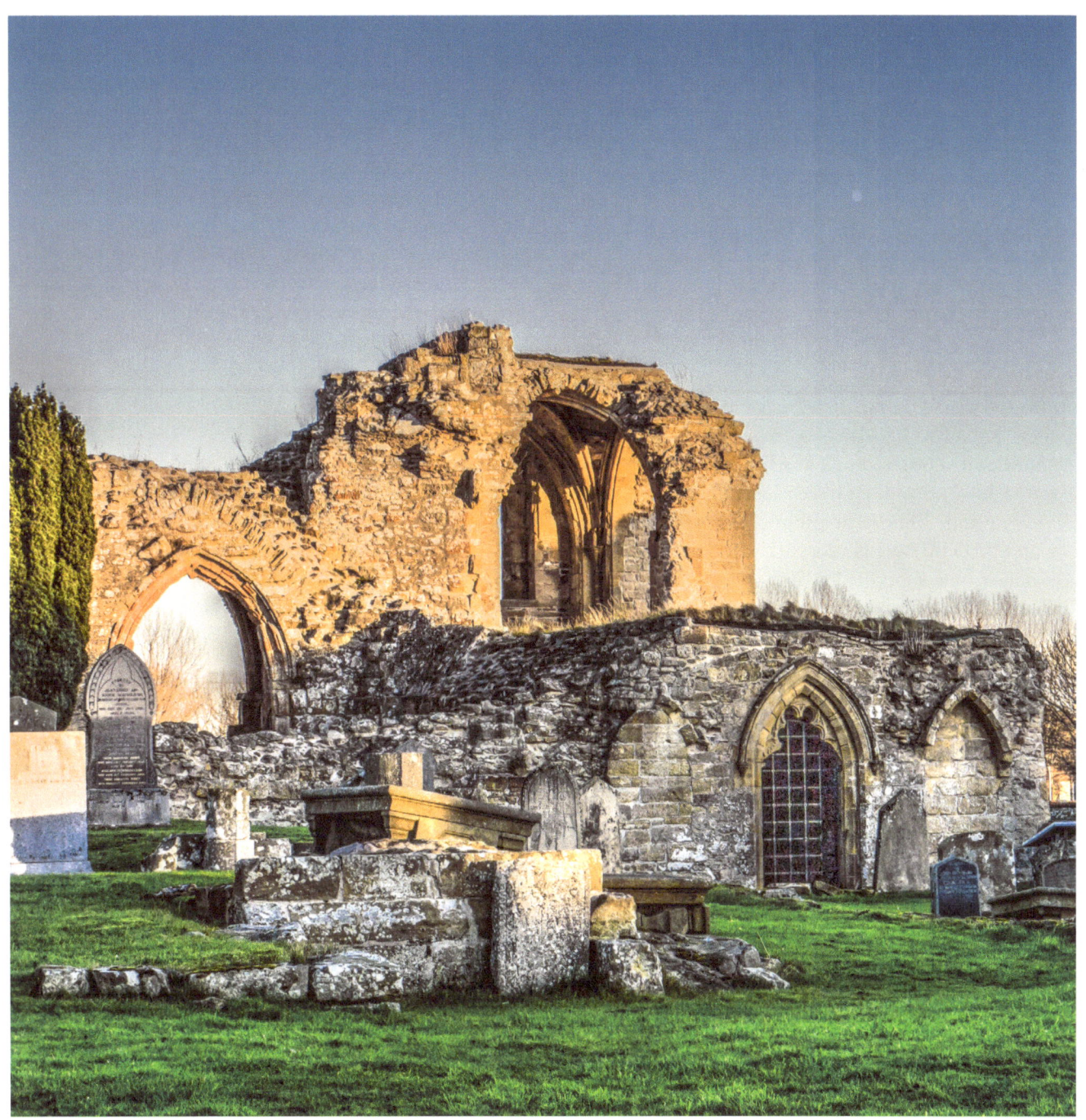

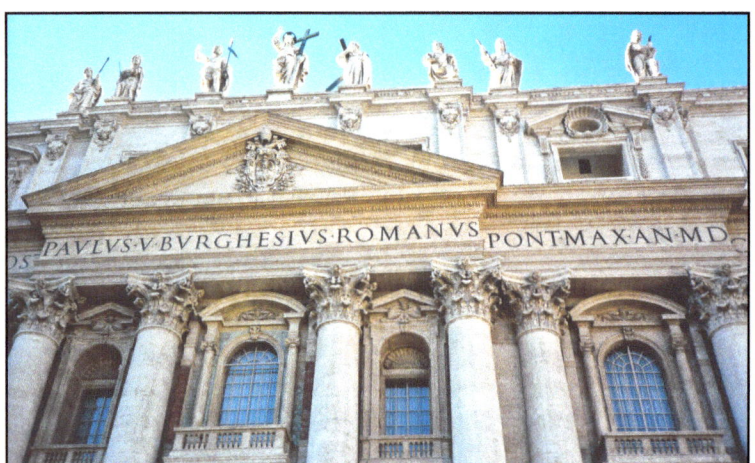

11th century North British Christianity had an Archbishop of York. Many, especially Bishop Maldovine of St Andrews, believed that Scotland should have its own Archbishop and not be ecclesiastically outranked from England. This Archbishopric of York had been set up in 735 by Pope Gregory III. Macbeth, who had previously been supported by Bishop Maldovine, was in full agreement with him on the matter.

Sometime after 1032 Macbeth married Gruoch the widow of Gillacomgain, who Macbeth had a hand in killing. It is thought that the slaying was partly revenge because cousin Gillacomgain was suspected of helping murder Finlay, Macbeth's father.

The marriage to Gillacomgain's widow brought together two royal lines of descent, which strengthened Macbeth's position against Malcolm II who still ruled Scotland at the time. Despite the delicate start, it seems their marriage was successful. Man and wife shared much in their lives. Macbeth also became a good father to Lulach son of Gruoch. The stepson became undisputed heir to Macbeth and many references to him often fail to include the "step" prefix.

Macbeth and Gruoch naturally shared their faith. From what records are available, it seems possible that Gruoch had the stronger affinity with the Church.

It is recorded that Macbeth, and probably his wife made a pilgrimage to Rome in 1050. *(Shown here is the 17th century entrance to St Peter's at the Vatican.)* The reason for making such a dangerous journey is thought to be so that Macbeth could position Scotland as a religious and civilised country alongside others whose Kings had already visited Pope Leo IX. It was likely to be on his agenda to discuss Scotland having an Archbishop. Unfortunately this didn't come about until the 15th century.

At some point Macbeth and Gruoch gave land to Culdee monks at Saint Serf's, an island on Loch Leven in Fife. The donation may have been made to ensure lots of prayers while on the pilgrimage. However, the date of the donation is not known. The main photograph is of the southern end of this island, where the monastery was sited. At around 1150, King David granted the island to the Augustinian Canons. What happened to the Culdee monks supported by Macbeth is uncertain.

The key historical significance of the long pilgrimage to Rome was that Macbeth knew that his position as King was secure. For this reason modern historians believe Macbeth to have been a decent and fair king. Scotland at the time of his visit to Europe was in a good state with little cause for civil or political unrest. It is therefore quite clear that Macbeth and his wife were done a grave injustice by Shakespeare's portrayal of them in the play.

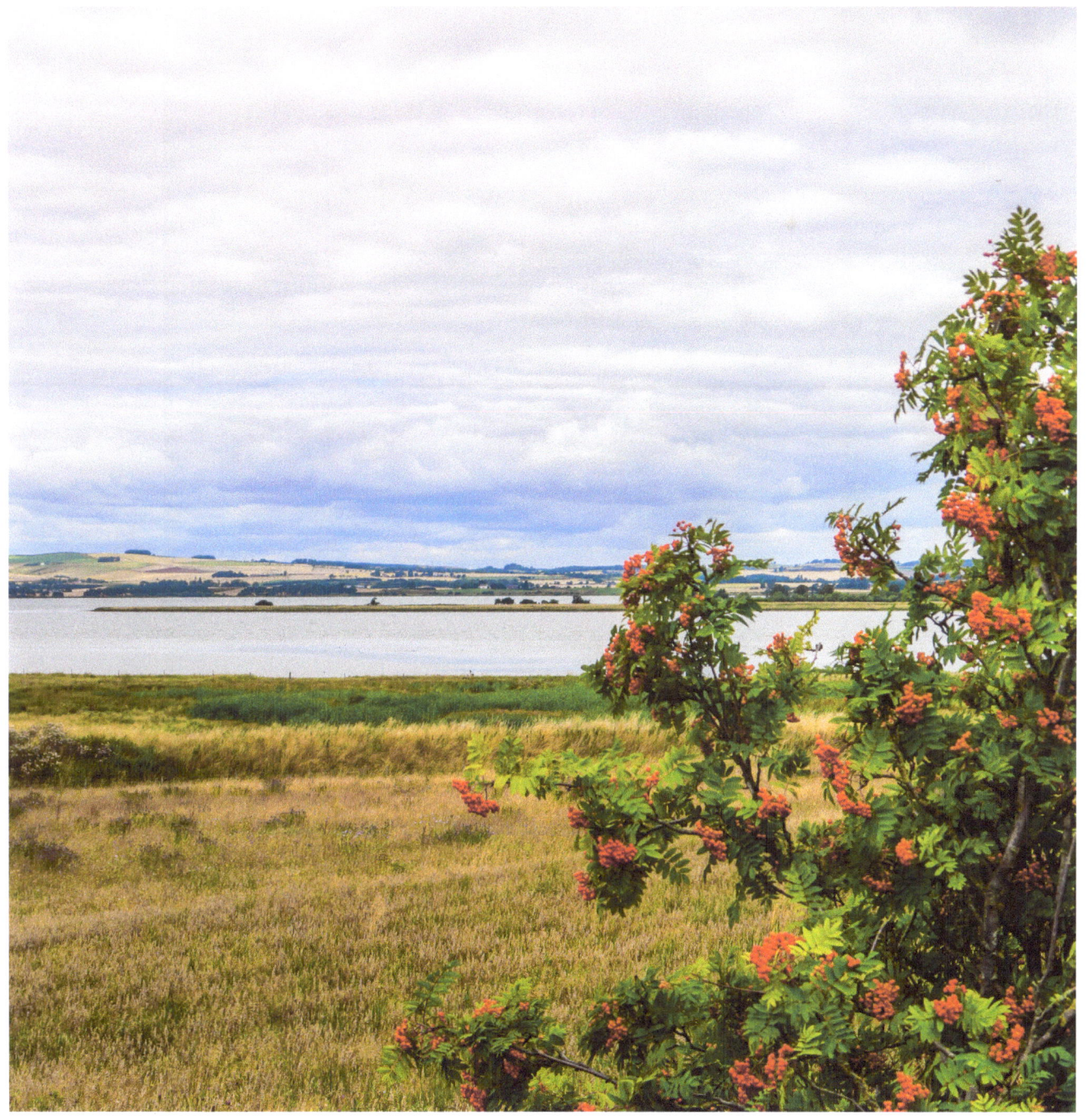

Palaces & Castles

11th Century Castles

Sadly there are no intact castles left from Macbeth's time. Most have been obliterated, left to crumble or have had new structures built upon them. It is therefore difficult to envisage what they might have looked like in the 11th century.

The fact that so little is left could perhaps indicate that they were made largely of materials prone to perishing or fire. Even where some ruins remain, such as Elgin Castle, their size is quite unimpressive. Perhaps castles such as those mentioned in the play were more like simple small fortified enclosures rather than what we understand by the term castle today.

Fortunately for the photographer there are sufficient buildings, ruins, sites, events and landscapes that have some Macbeth connections to warrant their inclusion in this section of the book.

Bamburgh Castle on the Northumberland Coast must be one of the most photogenic castles in the world. The photo here is the classic shot from the beach, with the castle up on the cliff and facing the North Sea. The siting and stature of the castle seems designed to intimidate potential raiders.

It is built on an outcrop of volcanic dolerite and was once the site of a Britons' fort known as Din Guarie. It could have been a regional capital until AD 547, when there is the first reference to a castle which was taken over by Ida, a ruler of Anglo-Saxons. It was passed onto an Anglo-Saxon wife called Bebba, from whom the name Benanburgh is said to be derived. This original fort was destroyed by Vikings in 993.

The current structure is based around a new castle built on the site by Normans. It has been added to and restored several times, with the most recent restoration work being carried out in the 19th century.

In 1971 Roman Polanski directed the film Macbeth and used the Bamburgh Castle as Dunsinane in the Shakespeare story. The choice is a little odd in that the North Sea adjoins Bamburgh Castle, while Dunsinane Hill is actually land-locked.

Bamburgh Castle was also used in 2015 for another film version of the play. This time it was meant to be Macbeth's own castle, which Shakespeare had placed in Inverness. The location choice for this film is slightly more appropriate than Polanski's in that both places give access to the North Sea. However, the mouth of River Ness flowing into the narrow end of the Moray Firth at Inverness bears little similarity to the open North Sea at Bamburgh.

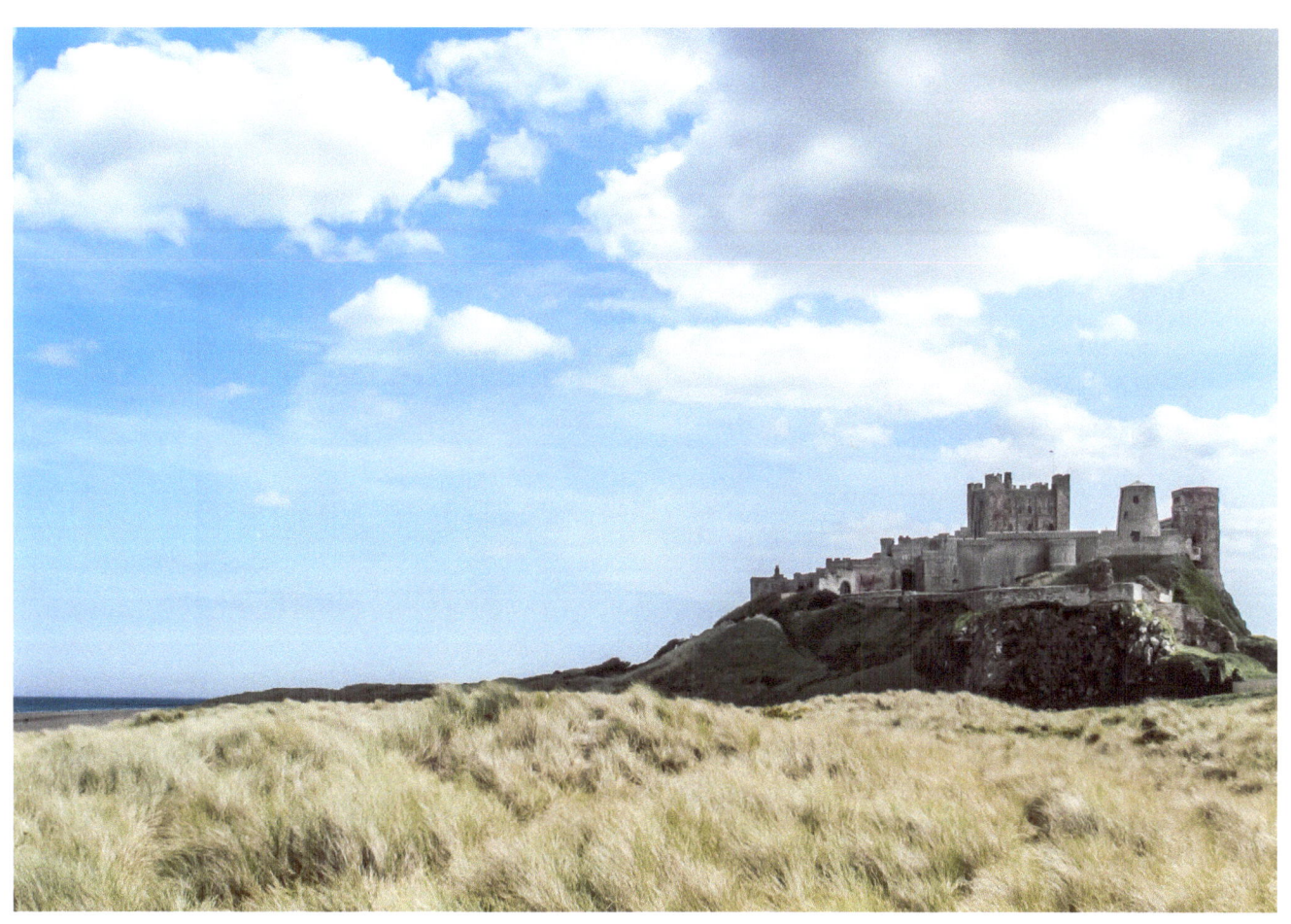

Elgin Castle

While Shakespeare failed to mention Elgin at all in his play, it does have some relevance to the life of Macbeth son of Finlay.

Though evidence is thin on the ground, it seems likely that a castle perched on Lady Hill in Elgin, with a number of wooden houses clustered around the foot the hill, existed at the time of Macbeth. This is certainly the view of Elgin Tourism sources and fits well with a brief Rotary-based history of the area. This states that Elgin was founded around the 10th century by a Norse general called Helgyn, from which the place name is derived.

While this seems all very plausible it should be mentioned that other sources have claimed that the name Elgin is derived from Gaelic. However, given the commonly acknowledged Norse influence on the lands around the Moray Firth at the time, the Gaelic argument for the source of the Elgin name appears weak.

It is also said that the Castle was a stronghold "at a very early date" and might have been an earthwork motte and bailey fortress in the late 11th century. It was elevated to the status of Royal Castle in the 12th century and was captured by King Edward 1st of England who stayed there in 1296 and in 1303.

Along with castles at Inverness, Nairn & Forres, the Elgin fortress was destroyed by Robert the Bruce in 1308 so that they could no-longer be used by English forces.

From the mound on which the castle ruins stand there is a 360 degree view of much of Moray with the Grampians and Highlands beyond.

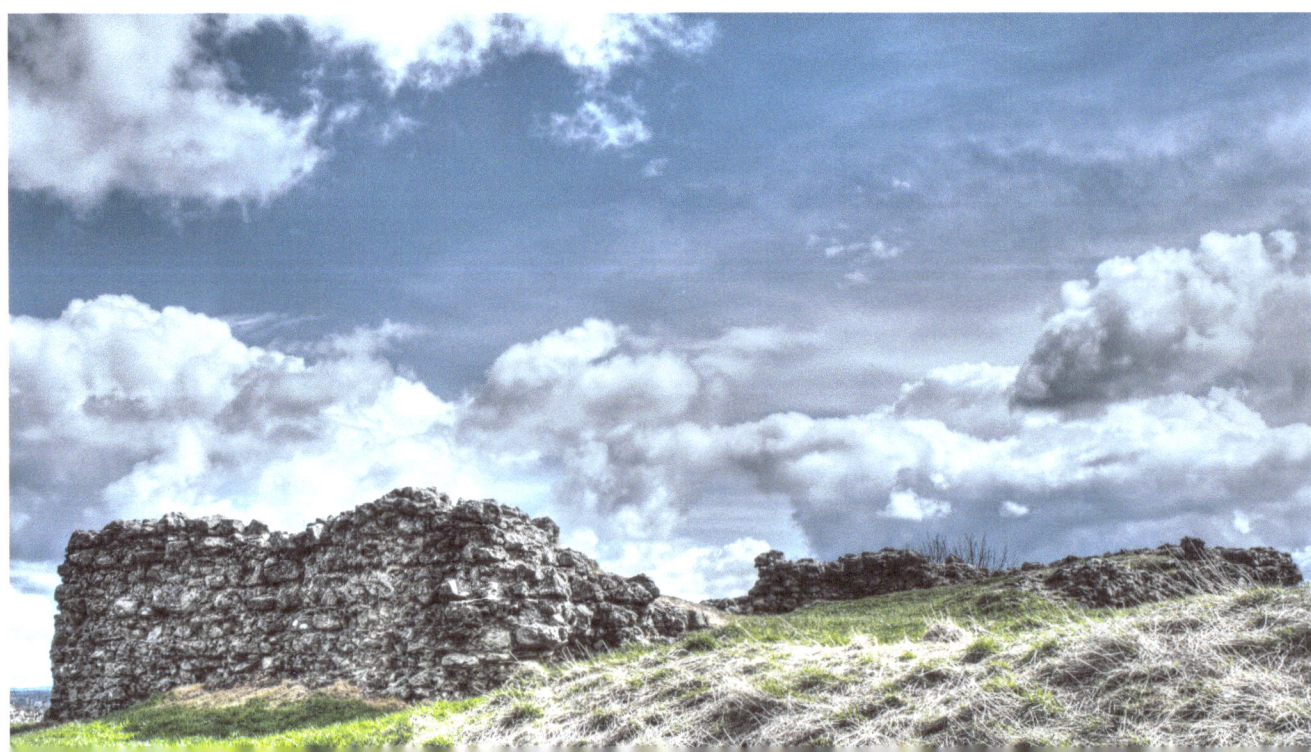

A few miles to the North East is Pitgaveny where Macbeth's forces are believed to have fought with those of King Duncan in 1040. It was the death of Duncan at this time which resulted in Macbeth assuming the Scottish crown.

There are differing accounts of where the battle took place, which forces took part, and how Duncan actually died. Some histories say he died at the hand of Macbeth, while others say was not even present on the battlefield.

One account even claims he died at the hands of his own army. However, according to Elgin Tourism sources, he was seriously wounded and then "Duncan was brought to Elgin where he died, almost certainly in the castle".

Elgin Castle may have been re-built sometime after the Robert the Bruce destruction, but is believed to have been completely unused, and left to ruin, since the 15th century.

Replacing the former imposing stature of the castle, and currently positioned beside it on the mound, is the Duke of Gordon Monument. This is the 1839 memorial to George, 5th Duke of Gordon who was normally styled as the Marquess of Huntly.

Why a monument should be erected to him in Elgin does not seem to be recorded. He was a noted MP, Chancellor of Marischall College Aberdeen and was the first commander of the Gordon Highlanders (founded by his father). That doesn't seem quite enough to explain why public subscription following a bequest by Morayshire Farmers Club should fund the scheme. Perhaps the folk of Elgin were simply envious of the Nelson Monument twelve miles away in Forres. It may also be possible that the large numbers of local men who were recruited into the Gordon Highlanders had influence on the decision.

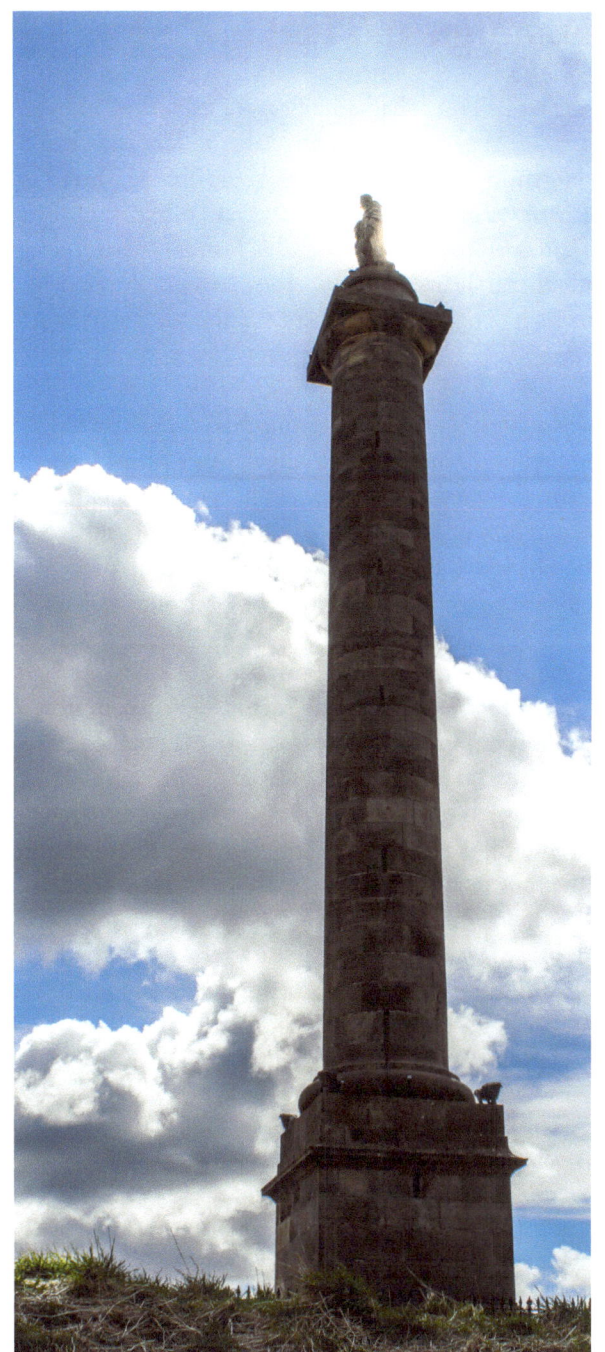

Bamburgh and Earl Siward

It was while Finlay had ambitions of extending his control in Scotland that King Malcolm II was defeated by Northumbrian forces led by Anglo-Saxon Uhtred at Durham. Uhtred's father was the Earl of Northumbria. He had preferred to remain in his fortress at Bamburgh while that fighting went on. The photograph opposite is the much extended and revised Bamburgh Castle as it is today.

It was a later Norseman-Northumbrian, Earl Siward, who had more direct and deadly contact with Macbeth. Siward had already strengthened his position by marrying the daughter of Ealdred, a later Earl of Bamburgh. When he killed the Earl's successor Eadulf in 1041 he acquired control of all Northumbria for himself.

That wasn't quite enough for Siward. His king-like power spread in England and included Northampton and Huntington. In the 1050's, with encouragement or possibly orders from Edward the Confessor, Siward turned his attention northwards and set about consolidating and extending influence in that direction. In the process he was to deal with Macbeth who, it had been alleged, had designs on westerly neighbour, Cumbria. It has also been said that Edward wished to see Malcolm Canmore on the Scottish throne, and it was to be Siward's role to ensure this outcome.

Whatever the true and full motivation, Siward headed north in pursuit of Macbeth. This resulted in the battle with Macbeth which is widely believed to have taken place at Dunsinane Hill in Perthshire. Macbeth survived that battle, and a victorious and plunder-laden (according to one account) Siward returned south.

Siward was so important to both English and Scottish history in the 11th century that even Shakespeare couldn't ignore the part he played. While some facts are vague, and although the writer used excessive artistic licence, he was correct in that (Siward's) Northumbrians fought Macbeth's forces in Perthshire.

Macbeth's great and powerful enemy Siward died in 1055. The following account of his death is taken from Historia Anglorum by Henry of Huntingdon;

> Siward, the stalwart earl, being stricken by dysentery, felt that death was near, and said;
>
> > *"How shameful it is that I, who could not die in so many battles, should have been saved for the ignominious death of a cow! At least clothe me in my impenetrable breastplate, gird me with my sword, place my helmet on my head, my shield in my left hand, my gilded battle-axe in my right, that I, the bravest of soldiers, may die like a soldier."*

He spoke, and armed as he had requested, he gave up his spirit with honour.

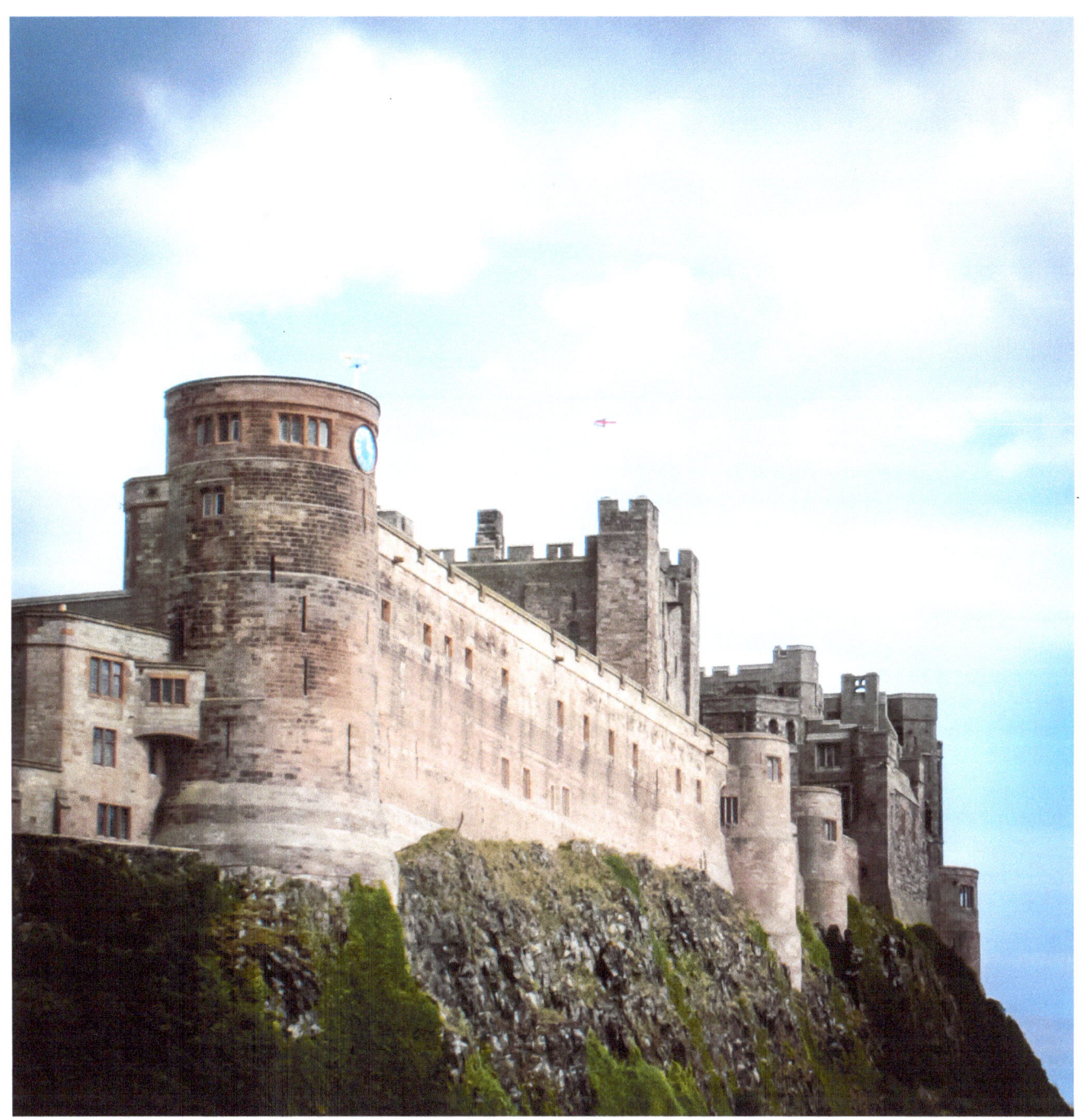

Inverness Castle

For many years historians believed that the Pict Kingdom of Fortrui was centred in Perthshire. However, more recent findings have resulted in the understanding that the "Capital" of Fortrui was somewhere further north in the lands just South of the Moray Firth. This area is often referred to in histories as Moray. That term can be confusing because of modern re-shaping and re-naming of administrative counties.

The historic area known as Moray includes parts of the modern Inverness-shire, Banffshire and Aberdeenshire along with all of Nairnshire and Morayshire. Inverness is at the western edge of old Moray, at the mouth of the River Ness. It is also at the narrowest point of the Moray Firth leading to the open North Sea. North of Inverness is the Black Isle and the Northern Highlands, which for centuries were dominated by the Norse. The siting of Inverness , known to be a Pictish stronghold, must have been a crucial part of the Pictish Fortrui lands.

Inverness is also situated at the Northern end of the Great Glen on an ancient valley, loch and river route from Ireland and Argyll to Moray and the East. Aside from its possible importance to the earlier Pictish Kingdom, it is likely to have been a major settlement during Macbeth's lifetime, when Gaelic parts of Scotland and Ireland were very closely linked.

The real Macbeth, son of Finlay, is likely to have at least known of the place and probably visited or passed through it. There is no evidence, though, that he ever resided in the place.

There has been a castle at Inverness on, or near, the same site by the River Ness since around 1100. This is, of course, after the death of the real Macbeth. The killing by Macbeth of guest King Duncan in Macbeth's home at Inverness Castle, is therefore factually impossible. It is a purely fictional scenario written by Shakespeare in his play.

The first castle was apparently of timber and turf construction. It is believed that Robert the Bruce destroyed this castle. To replace it a stone castle was probably built during the early 15th century. This structure met a similar fate to the first when it was blown up by Bonnie Prince Charlie during the Jacobite rebellion of 1746.

The current castle, shown here, was built in 1836 by architect William Burn. It is used today by the Inverness Sheriff Court and, when built, it also included a jail..

The combination of colours in this photo is quite genuine. It was taken with the sun low in the sky on an April afternoon while dark clouds loomed in the East, towards Moray.

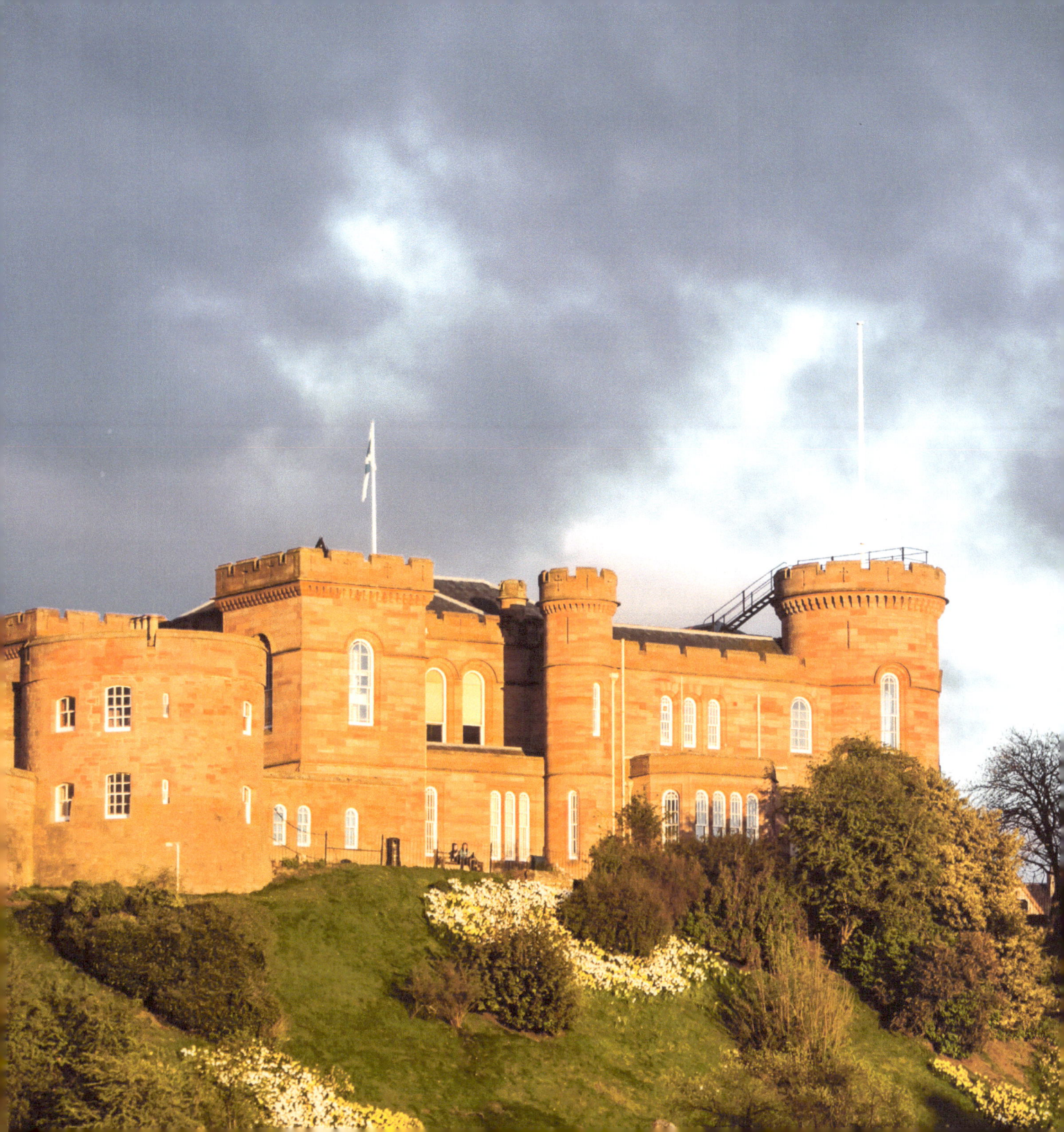

Thane of Glamis, or Cromarty?

Glamis is the first place mentioned in Shakespeare's play, of which the Macbeth, son of Finlay, was not a Thane. There is a connection though with the complicated story of 11th century Scottish succession. Malcolm II died at a lodge in Glamis from wounds after doing battle, perhaps with forces allied to Macbeth. As Malcolm actually won that battle his death did not, however, result in Macbeth's instant elevation, The title of King of Scotland passed instead to Malcolm's grand-son Duncan.

The magnificent Castle at Glamis, pictured here, was first built by 1376, when King Robert II granted it to Sir John Lyon. It has also seen many changes since that date. Of course it could never have been the home of the real Macbeth.

According to some histories and tourist web sites, Macbeth was Thane of Cromarty. This initially seems improbable as the area, according to evidence from Portmahomack further north, was likely to be under Caithness and Norse jurisdiction in those days.

At Finlay's request, and maybe as a training for a higher ranking, a young Macbeth could have been involved in the occasional adventure across the Moray Firth to the Black Isle. An ambitious Finlay may well have considered its lands as part of his Moray.

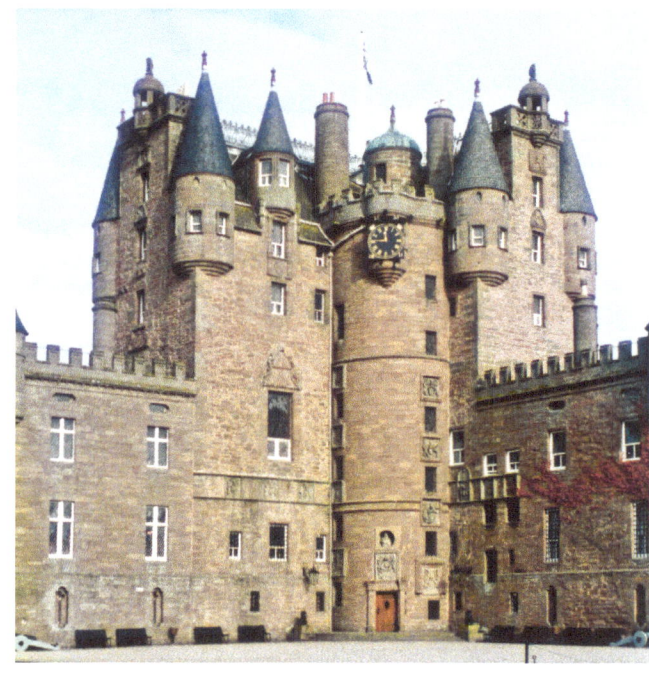

The larger photo is taken from Rosemarkie Beach which is on the South edge of Black Isle facing towards Cromarty.

Rosemarkie is near a very narrow part of the Moray Firth, marked these days by Fort George on the south side and Chanonry Point Lighthouse on the north. As such, it was probably the quickest route for Finlay and Macbeth to cross from Scottish-Gael Moray into Caithness-Norse Black Isle.

Over many centuries the Moray Firth has been a major seaway used by Picts, Romans, Gaels, Scots and of course Norsemen. It is also very likely that French, Saxons and Dutch later used it to visit and trade with those living and working the lands on the South side of the Firth. The importance of the Moray Firth in terms of North Scottish history cannot, therefore, be over-stressed.

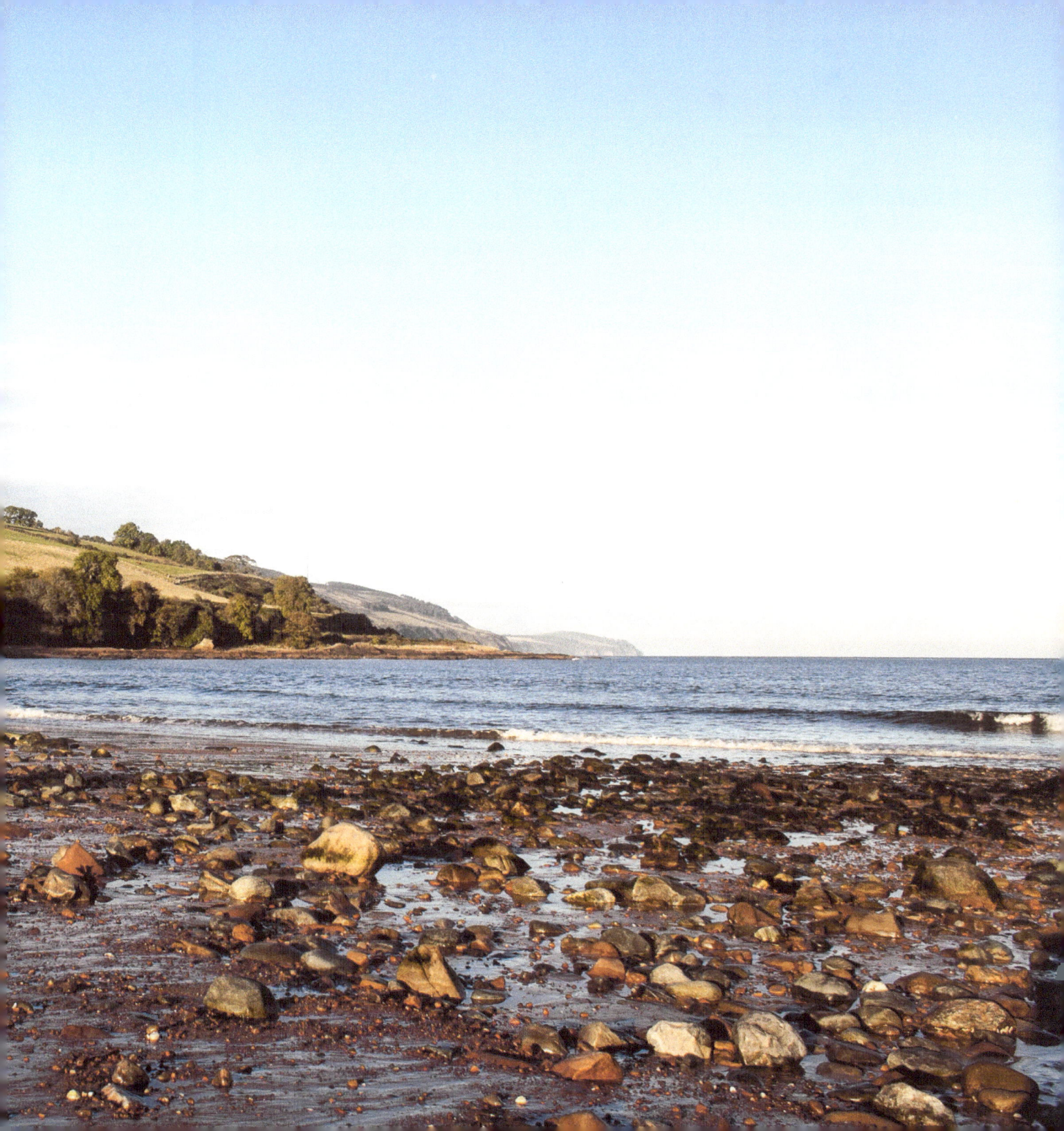

Torridon Fort - Burghead

Without doubt there was significant activity around the ports and Christian centres on the northern side of the Moray Firth in the 11th century. However, it was the south side and the lands of Moray that attracted most trade, settlement and territorial dispute. The Moray Firth ports played a huge part in the story of the true Macbeth, not least because King Duncan's forces arrived by sea to try and subdue him. Yet sea travel gets no mention by Shakespeare in his play. This is perhaps indicative that he never actually visited the area. Had he done so he would surely have realised how vital the sea was to travellers, adventurers, traders, armies and invaders of the times.

The fact that foreigners frequently visited Moray by sea, not always with friendly intent, led to the need for defensive structures. Canmore, the on-line catalogue of Scottish archaeology, includes a 19th century reference to a castle at Nairn, believed to have been "extant in the time of Malcolm 1". The fortress would most likely have been built by Picts as part of a defence against viking attack. It was described as "a tower on a peninsula of extraordinary height" and the remains were claimed to be still visible in the 18th century. Unfortunately, more recent surveys have failed to find any evidence of this structure.

Time has been a little kinder to Burghead Fort, about 18 miles miles east of Nairn. It has been referred to as the largest Iron Age Fort in Britain and was originally known as Torridon. It was constructed by Picts around AD 400 and it was known to be subject to Viking raids in the 8th and 9th centuries.

The Burghead Visitor Centre web-site states that it was captured in 884 by Sigurd the Powerful, the Norse Earl of Orkney. It is thought to have been destroyed by fire around the 10th century. During the clearances in the early 19th century a planned village was built there and the place was renamed Burghead. Unfortunately much of the fortress ruins were lost in the process. Some stones from the fort were re-used and new buildings were built over other ruins.

Fortunately, some later excavation has taken place and the full historical significance of the fort has been recognised. It has fairly recently been claimed that Torridon was such a vast fortification that it must have been a prominent Pictish centre. Historians have recently debated an understanding that the Pictish Kingdom of Fortrui was based in Perthshire. As a result it is now commonly held that it was based further north. Torridon may well have been the "capital" of Fortrui.

The fort used a promontory, jutting into the Moray Firth, to great advantage with fortifications built into the earth. The photo shows one edge of the promontory with a cliff-like face hanging over the sea. At the top left of the photo can be seen some of the stone work of the Pictish fortification.

The fortress was reduced to ruins by Macbeth's time in the 11th century. It is not clear whether Torridon was permanently occupied between then and the building of Burghead in the 19th century. Perhaps, as some suggest happened at Nairn, some Norse settlement took place for at least some of that time.

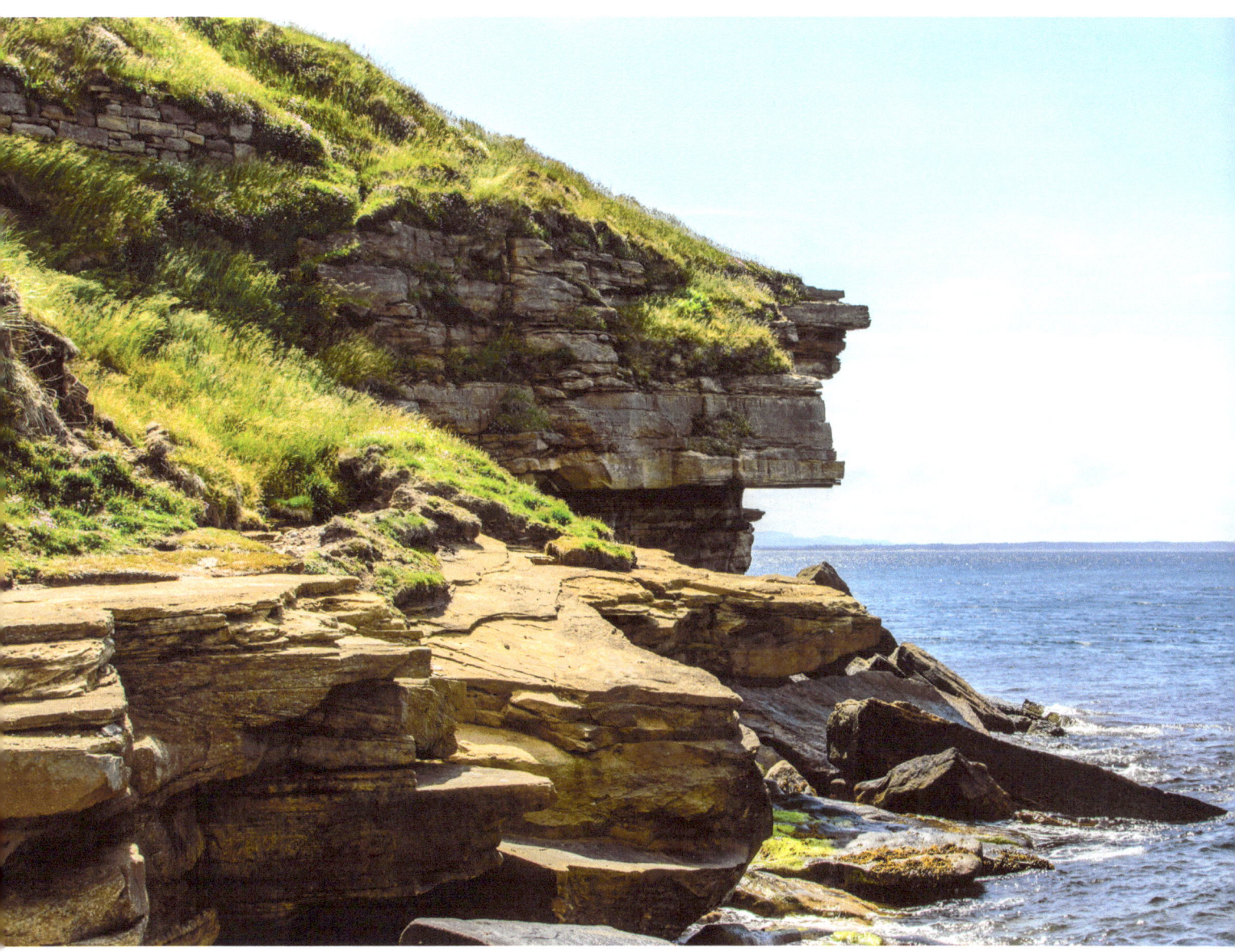

Cawdor Castle

Unlike many castles, Cawdor surpasses expectations. While it has a sinister name associated with that of a murderous fictional character, the castle still proves to be somehow more dramatic than expected. It is the sort of castle that block-buster movie producers would love and could use for practically anything from historical movies to murder mystery drama.

The earlier name for the area is Calder. This is derived from Cale, meaning wood, and Dor representing water. Calder therefore means woods between waters, possibly being the area between the River Nairn and the Moray Firth. Cawdor is actually a phonetic spelling of Calder.

As already mentioned, Macbeth was never Thane of Cawdor. The castle was not built until long after his time. The first recorded Thane of Cawdor was Donald in 1295. However the exact date that building of the castle started is not known. The stonework has led some to believe it was about 1380. That a building licence was issued in 1454 has led others to accept that later date.

Nevertheless, many tourists visit Cawdor Castle because of a connection with the Thane invented by Shakespeare. Such influx of visitors prompted the late 6th Earl of Cawdor, who died in 1993, to have stated "I wish the Bard had never written his damned play!"

As mentioned earlier, the castle is currently occupied by Lady Angelika, the Dowager Countess of Cawdor, and under her auspices it has deservedly become one of the top tourist venues in Scotland.

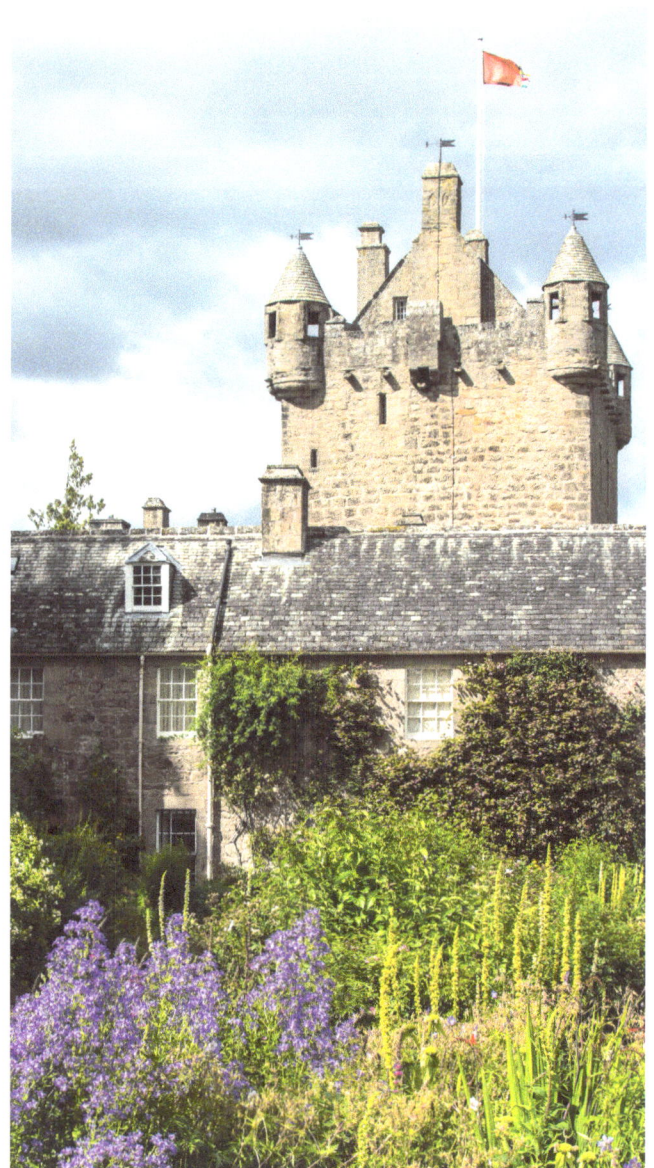

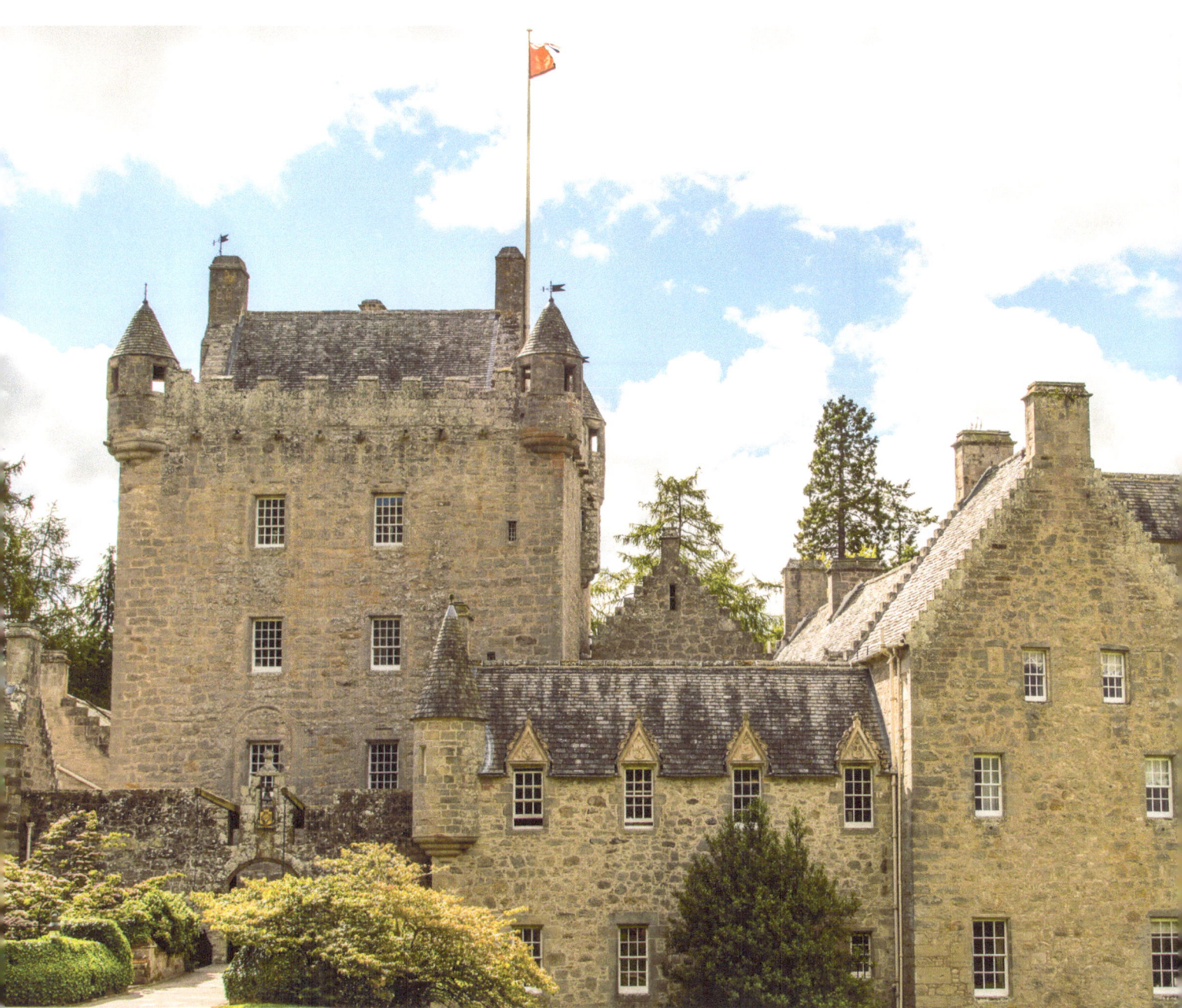

Brodie Castle

The first Brodie Castle was built in 1567 by Clan Brodie but destroyed in 1645 by Lewis Gordon, the 3rd Marquess of Huntly.

The current building, dating from 1824, is largely the work of William Burn. The earlier destruction was incomplete as the original 16th century tower remains a significant part of the building.

The Brodie family transferred the castle to the National Trust for Scotland in the late 20th century.

While Brodie Castle did not exist in Macbeth's time but is worthy of inclusion here because it is an attractive and significant Castle in the heart of Moray.

It is also just a couple of miles from the Macbeth Hillock, a rumoured site of the "desert place" used by Shakespeare's witches in the play.

Forres, where Shakespeare placed King Duncan's palace, is only four miles to the East.

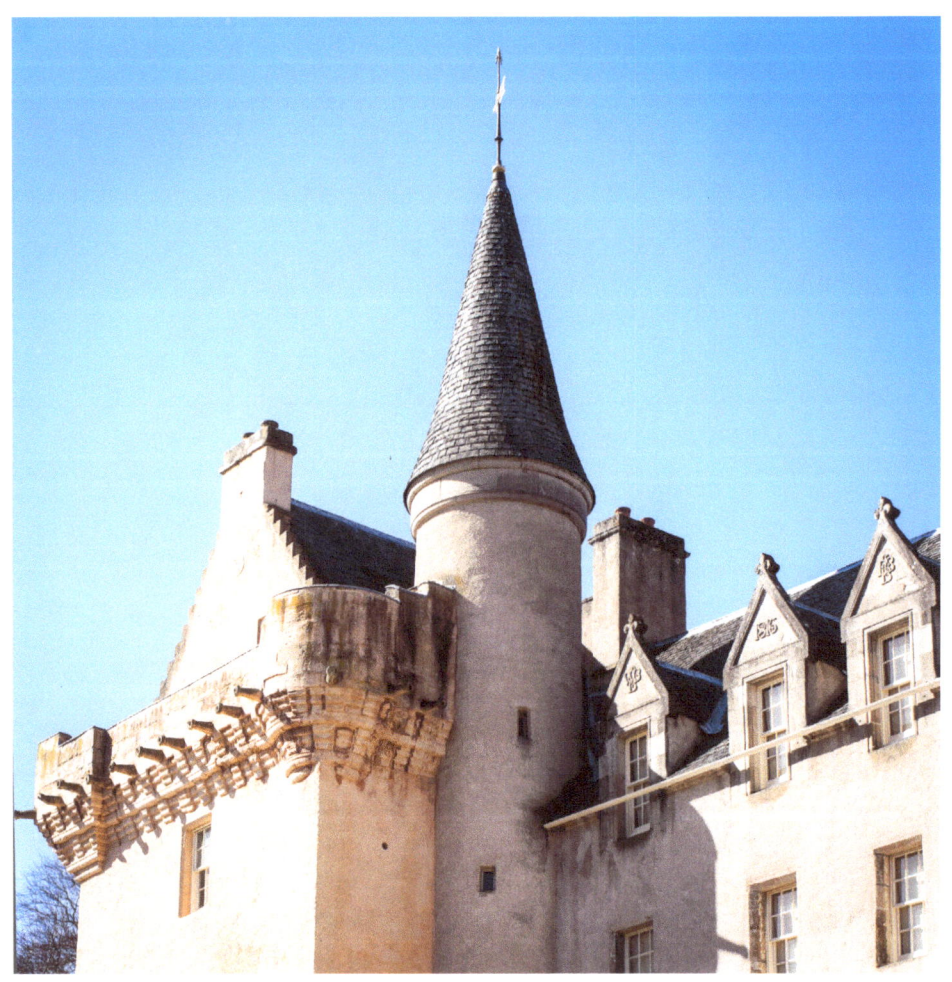

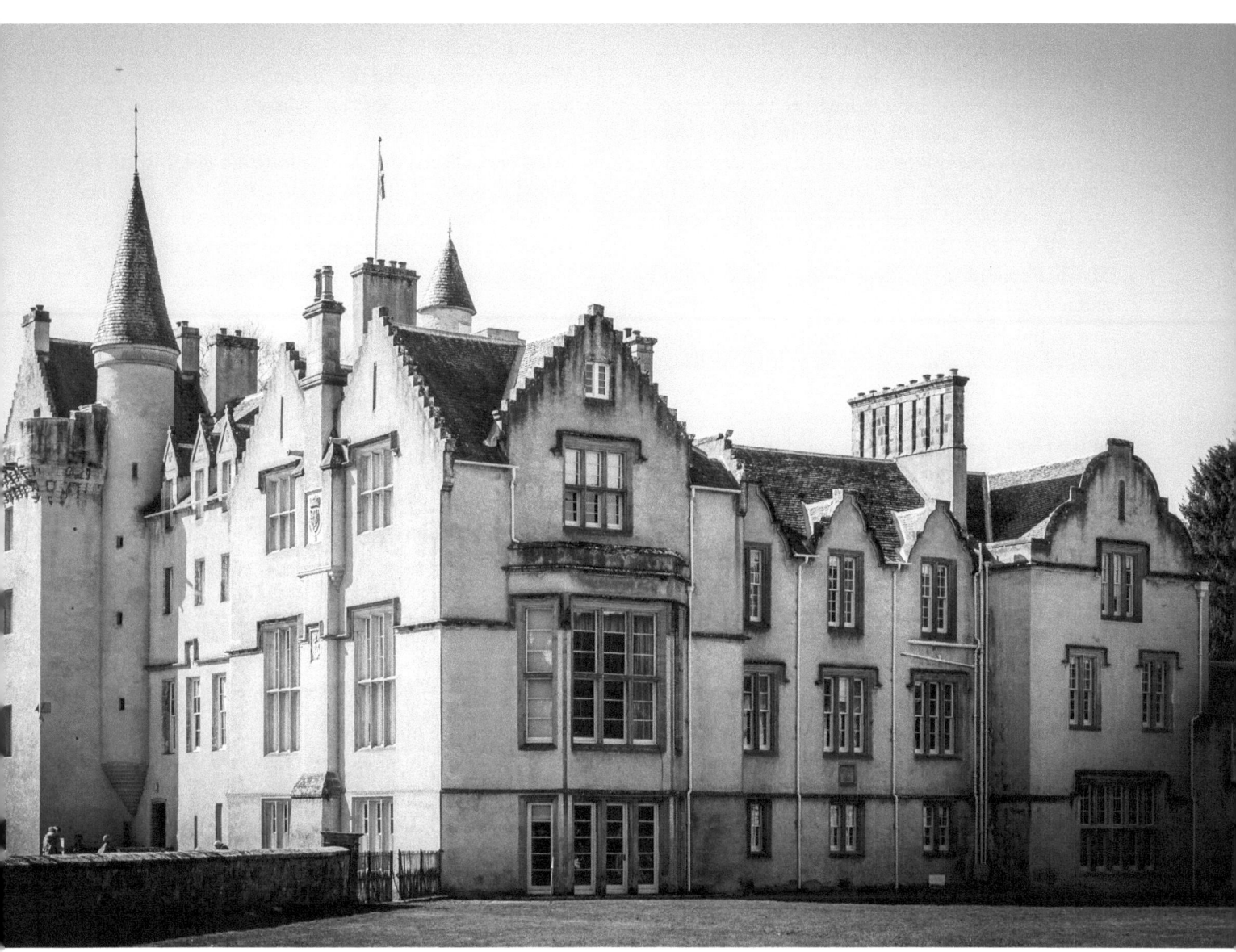

Macduff's Castle

A castle is believed to have been built at a site near East Wemyss in Fife in the 11th century at the time when Macbeth, son of Finlay, was King of Scotland. Furthermore it is thought to have been built by the powerful family Macduff, Earls of Fife. Unfortunately the original castle is long gone. The ruin seen here, and now known as Macduff's Castle, was built in the 14th century by Macduff decendents, the Wemyss family.

Macduff appears in The Scottish Play as a Thane of Fife and nobleman of Scotland. The real Macduff was not a Thane, but probably a Mormaer, that is, a top-ranking local administrator ranked second only to the King of Scotland.

In the play, Macbeth fears that Macduff knows everything regarding the murder of King Duncan. Macbeth then murders Macduff's family. The play ends with a revengeful Macduff killing Macbeth at the Battle at Dunsinane. The reality is that, aside from the fact that the true Macbeth was not killed by anyone at Dunsinane, there is no evidence that the Earl of Fife and he ever met.

The Gaelic word "dubh" meaning "black" is the origin of the name Duff which thus goes back before Macbeth's days. It is possible that the King Dubh of Forres, whose life may have given inspiration for Shakespeare's use of witches, would have been an ancestor of the later Mormaers of Fife.

The coastal area of Wemyss is well known for its number of coastal caves and that some have been used for shelter for many centuries. This is because Pictish carvings have been found in some of them.

The smaller photo below shows one such small cave just beneath Macduff's Castle. Some have suggested that Wemyss caves inspired the "desert" meeting place used, according to Shakespeare, by witches in Macbeth.

It has been alleged that Shakespeare did visit Scotland including some of the places where the play is set. There is no evidence of such visits and, even if they did occur, it is doubtful if the Wemyss caves would have been as well known and on his itinerary, at that time.

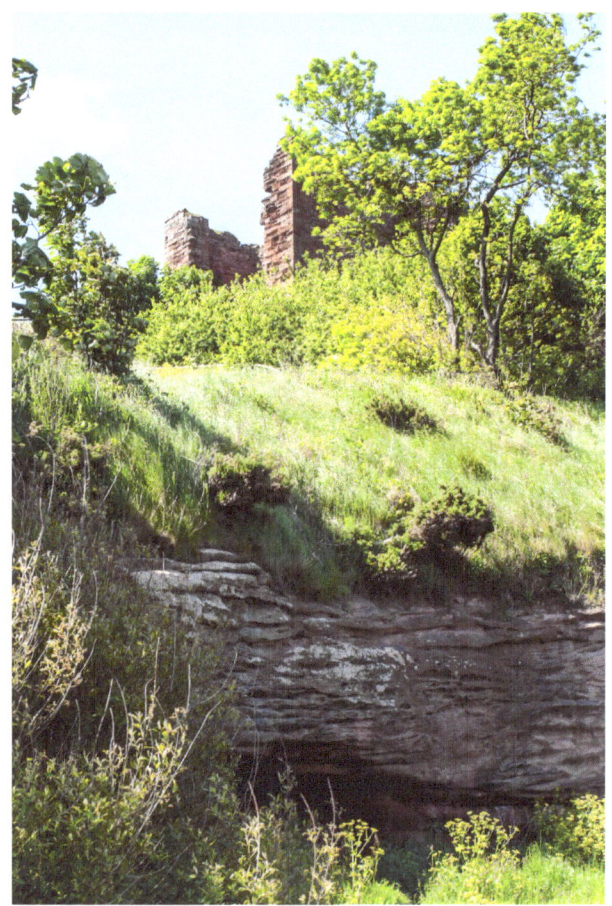

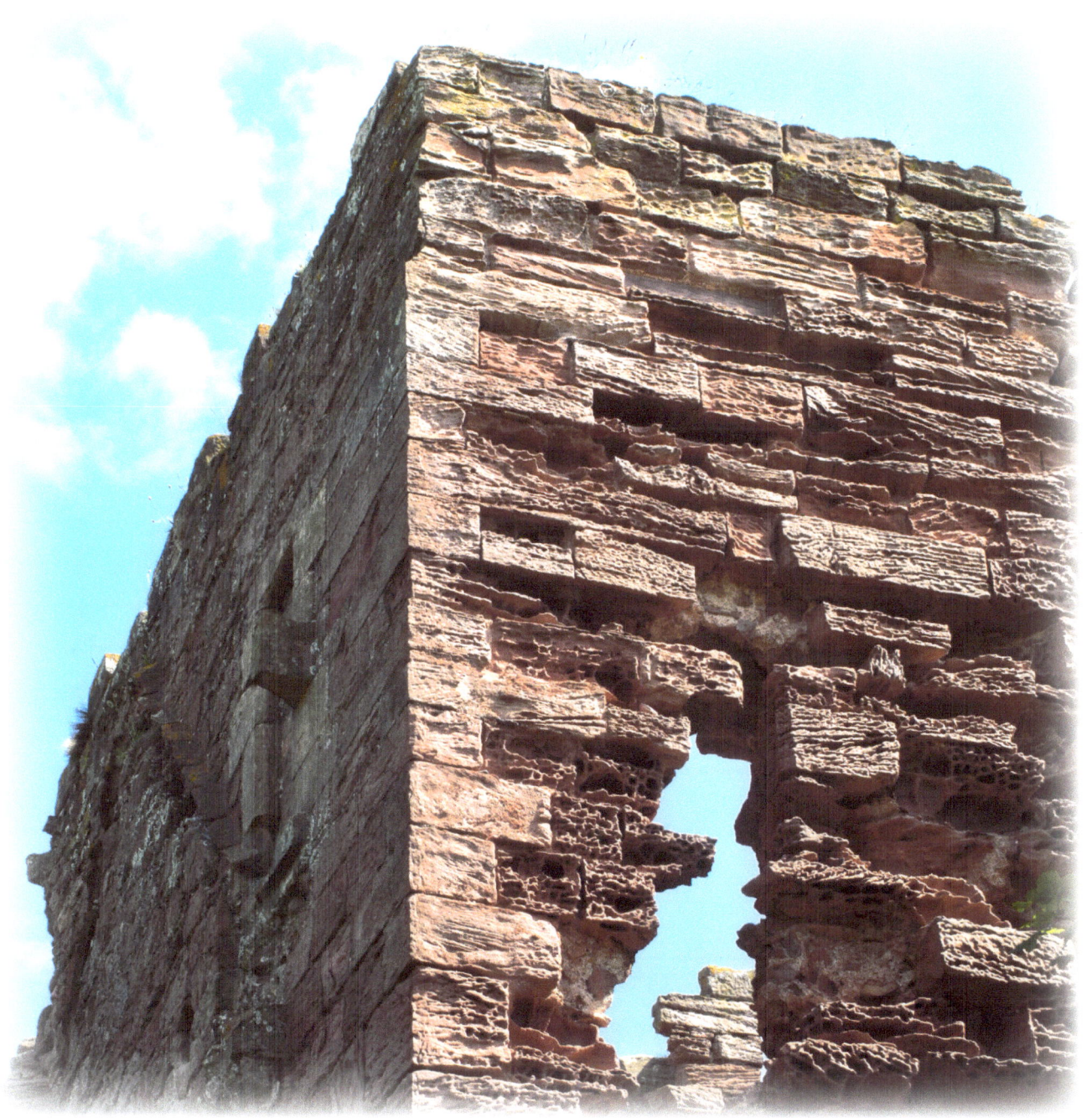

Battles, Death & Succession

Sueno's Stone - Forres

Sueno's Stone photographed on these pages is at Forres in Morayshire and is the largest known Pictish sculptured stone. On one side is a large cross and the other includes scenes of fighting and killing, dead and decapitated bodies.

While the stone is clearly a form of memorial it is far from certain who erected it or exactly what it depicts.

It is generally accepted that erection took place in the later decades of the first millennium, probably in the 9th century. The Undiscovered Scotland website offers three explanations;

> a) that it represents the defeat of the Picts by Scots under Kenneth Mac Alpin in 841;
>
> b) it signifies a battle involving the forces of the Norse King Swein Forkbeard (or "Sueno") against Scots;
>
> c) it represents an actual historical encounter between Norse and Picts, or the battle known to have been fought at Forres in 966 by King Dubh (Duff) for control over Moray.

This stone shows vividly just how long men have been fighting and killing over the lands by the Moray Coast. It also means that Shakespeare was being largely consistent with this bloody past by starting the Macbeth play in Forres.

There is ample evidence that the area was known to the Romans. Claudius Ptolemaeus (Ptolemy) produced a map of the Roman World which includes this part of Northern Scotland.

Evidence of Roman forts have also been found in the area at Birnie, Cawdor and Alves. Whether the Romans ever had serious plans to conquer the peoples of Northern Scotland is doubtful. There is certainly no evidence that they did. It seems more likely that their presence was, like other seagoing peoples at the time, for trade only purposes. The Rivers Lossie, for Elgin, and Findhorn, for Forres, would have played a significant part in such trade.

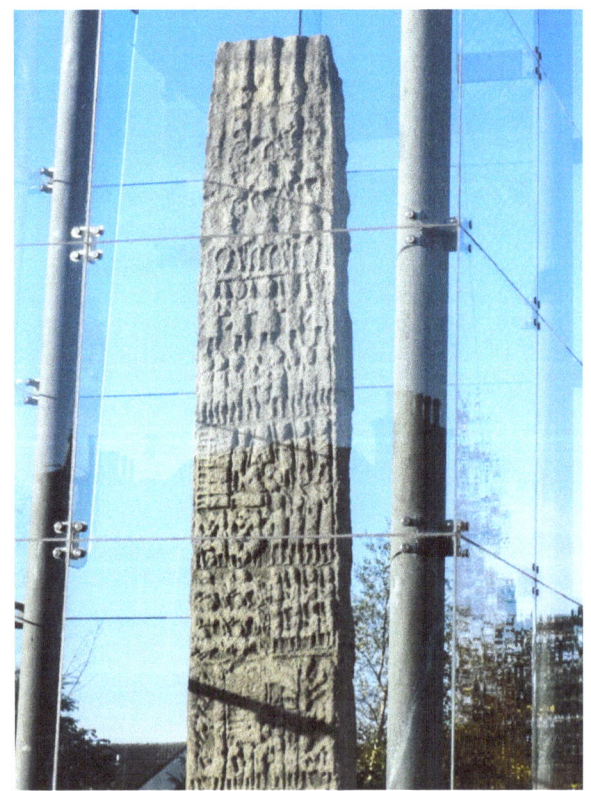

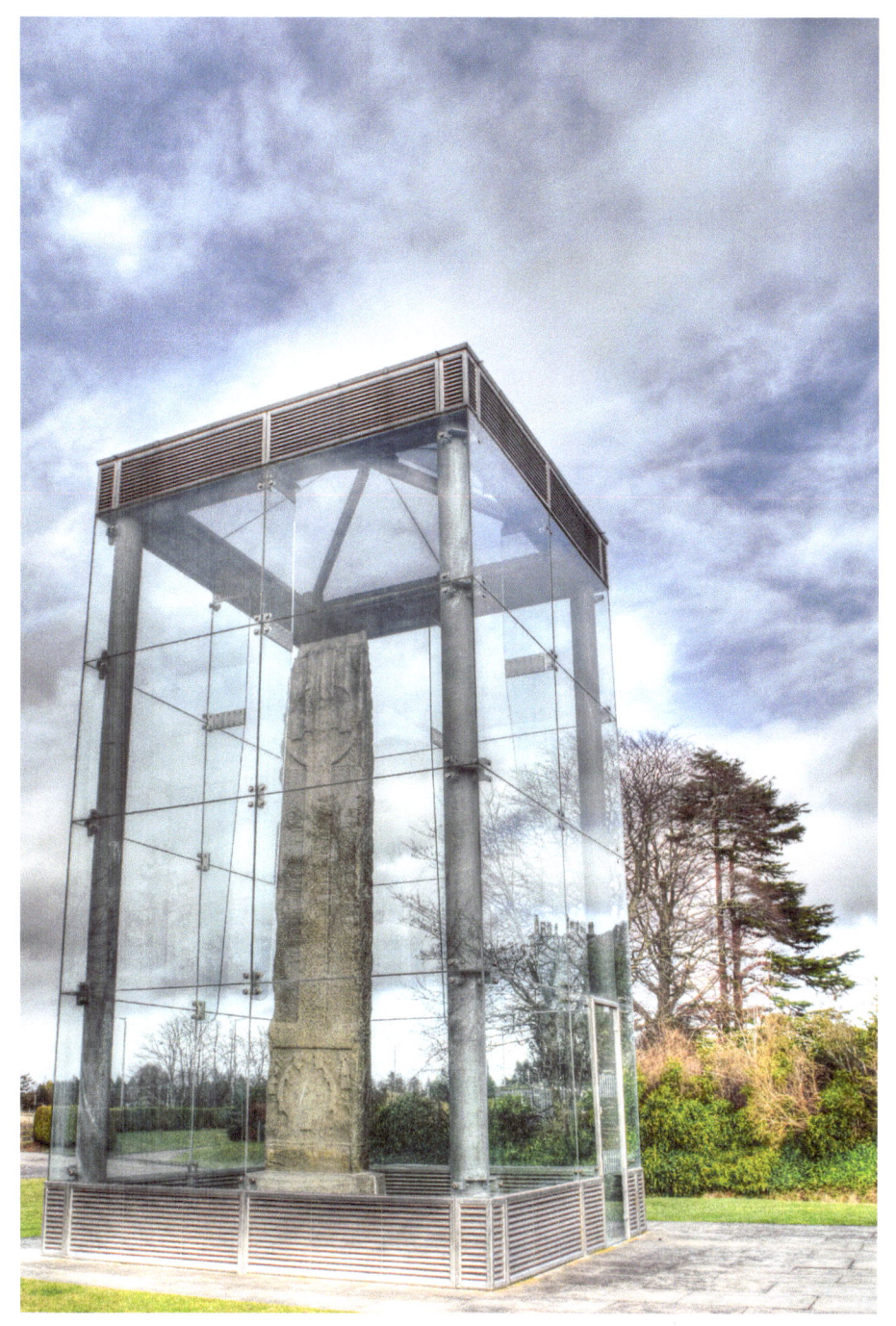

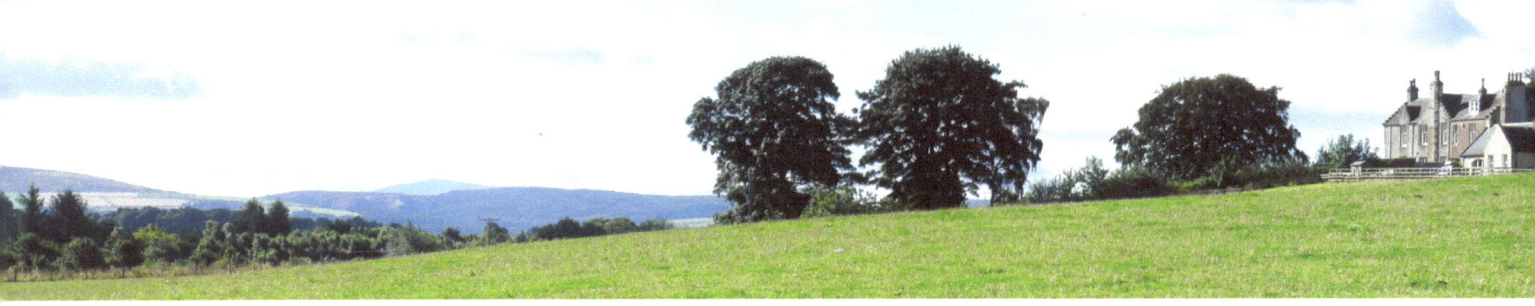

Pitgavney, Loch Spynie & Spynie Palace

When Duncan returned defeated after his failed raid on Durham, he chose a spot by the Loch of Spynie in Moray to do battle with Macbeth, the strong contender to his throne. The battle site, just outside today's Elgin, is known as Pitgavney. Unfortunately the actual site is not currently marked or mapped.

The land has changed much over the centuries. Loch Spynie, in Macbeth's day, was easily navigable to the sea and it is very probable that Duncan's forces arrived by that route in sea-going craft. However, due to drainage and silting, the size of the Loch is much reduced now and one can only guess today at where the ships landed and the battle took place.

All detail of the battle is obscure. While it is known to have taken place in 1040 not much else is certain. Some tales claim that Macbeth killed Duncan in the battle and that Duncan's bones were buried at Elgin Cathedral. In one account the battlefield was said to be within sight of Elgin Cathedral. To confuse matters further, there are accounts of a Battle of (nearby) Burghead in 1040, which involved Orkney-based Norse and Irish troops. It is also said that Duncan may have been killed at Burghead, in battle, or by his own army.

On balance it seems probable that Pitgavney and Burghead are different names for the same battle which, one way or another, proved fatal for Duncan. His death, in turn, also resulted in Macbeth assuming the throne.

The peaceful image above is a group of buildings currently having the address Pitgavney. As the ground falls away and below those buildings it reaches the place where Loch Spynie would have reached in 1040. This is where some local historians believe the battle took place.

The photo of Pitgavney was taken from the grounds of Spynie Palace, part of which is seen on the opposite page. Spynie Palace, along with Saint Andrews, are the largest surviving medieval bishop's houses in Scotland.

The palace towers, had they existed in 1040, would have given grandstand views of the battle below. However the palace was not established as the home of the bishops of Moray until the 12th century. At that time the route to open sea, by means of the Loch, came right up to the hill on which the palace stands. The outlines of ancient berths for fishing and merchant vessels can still be made out in the low level meadows.

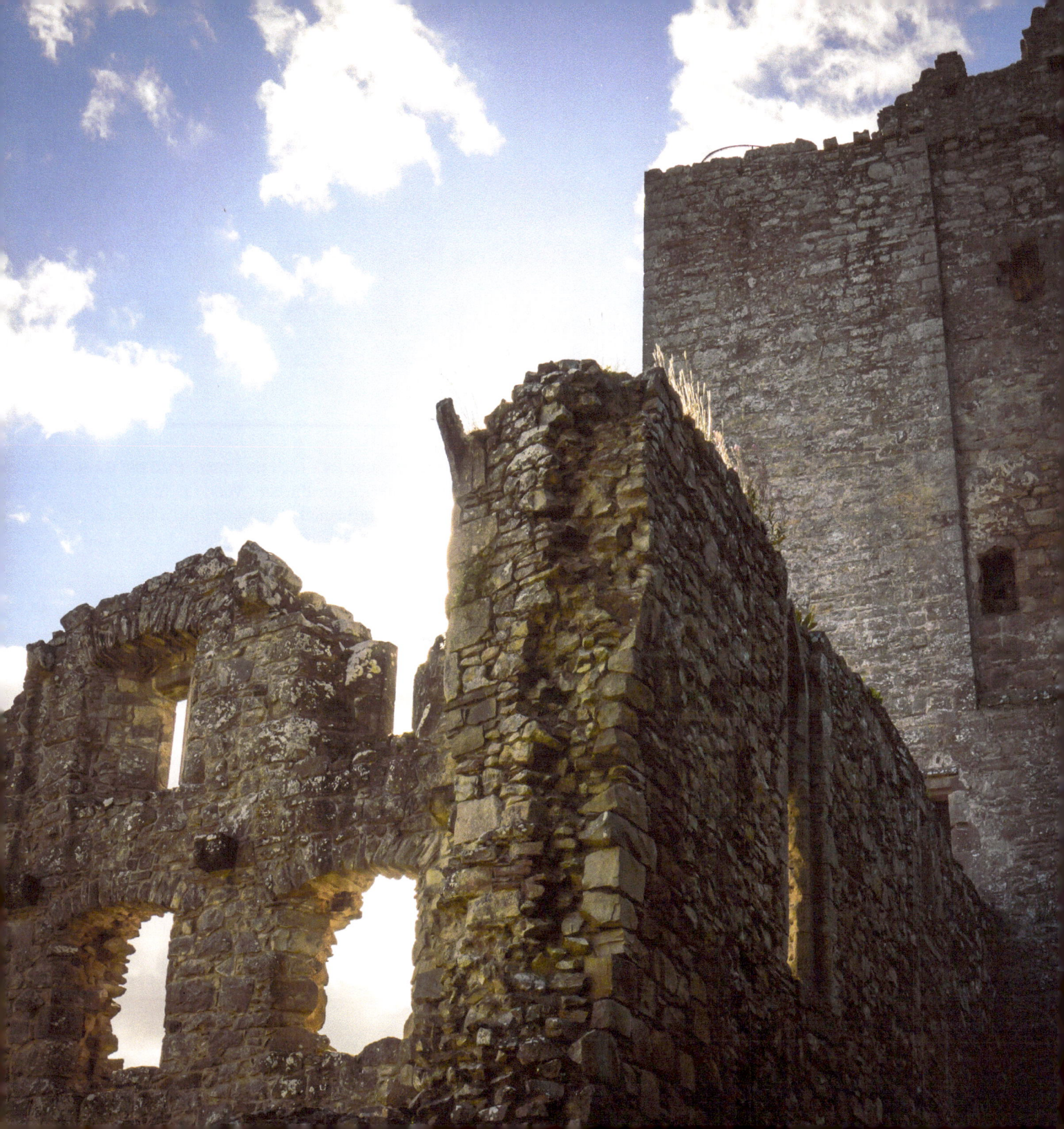

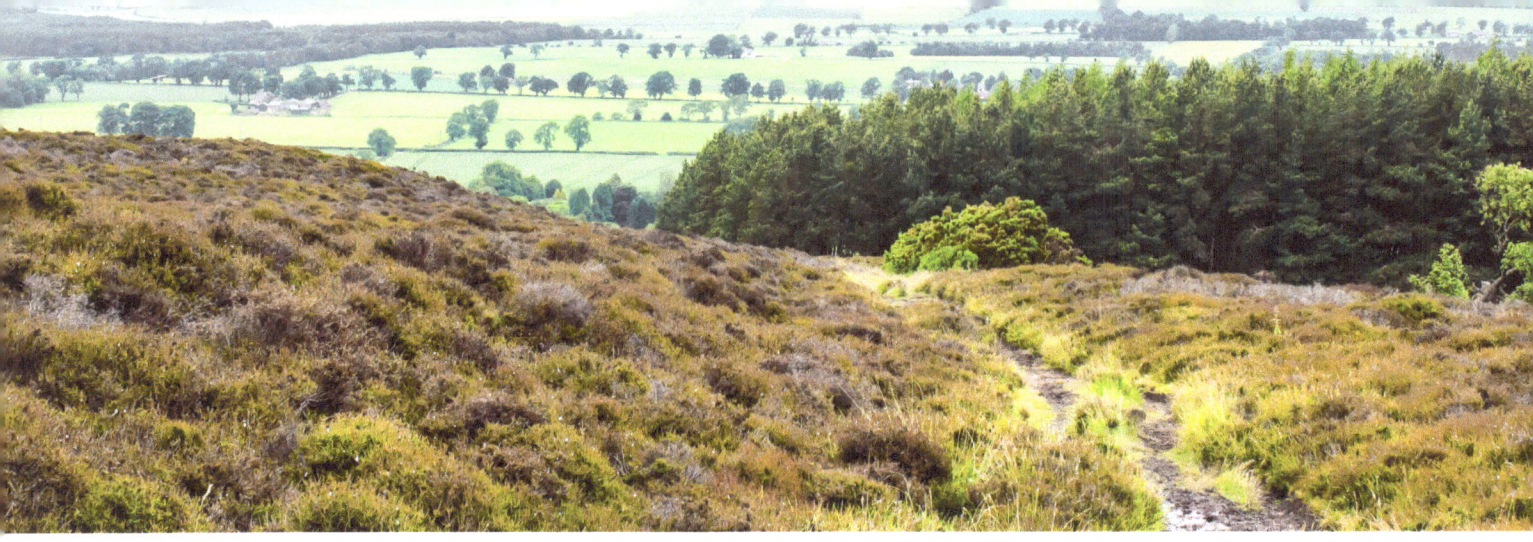

Dunsinane Hill - Perthshire

Dunsinane Hill near Collace has a ruined fort at its peak. It has commanding views of lowlands around and is in an easily defensible position. The fort is above the tree-line of surrounding, and comparatively recent, conifers. Remnants of the ancient Birnam Wood are today about 13 miles from the hill.

The photograph gives a reasonable idea of the commanding views from the hill. It also shows the edge of some recent woods below. These would have included oak and stretched well beyond, to Birnam, in Macbeth's time.

Some maintain that Shakespeare must have had personal knowledge of places such as Dunsinane in order to write his play with some geographical and climatic accuracy. However, is seems more likely that the majority of his tale of Macbeth was taken from Holinshed's Chronicles which were published in 1587.

It was these chronicles which first mentioned the use of camouflage taken from Birnam Wood to move forces stealthily up Dunsinane Hill. More modern histories confirm that there was indeed a battle in the area, and most probably at Dunsinane.

Earl Siward had plans to extend his Northumbrian Earldom. He also wished to end the threat posed by Macbeth who understandably wished to protect his own land, Scotland. So in 1054 Siward headed north with an army in search of Macbeth.

On hearing that Northumbrians had crossed Lothian, Macbeth is thought to have retreated, hoping that Siward would tire of searching for him. Macbeth passed through Scone heading for the hills between Perth and Dundee. Siward followed and Macbeth had to establish a defensive position, most probably at Dunsinane. He reluctantly did battle with Siward on 27 July 1054. Many died on both sides and Macbeth's forces suffered defeat in the battle. Nevertheless he survived. It is unclear, especially after battle victory, how Siward failed to kill or capture Macbeth.

"Macbeth shall never vanquish'd be until Great Birnam Wood to high Dunsinane Hill shall come against him."

Birnam Wood is clearly identified on Ordnance Survey maps and is about 12 miles north of Perth. The village of Birnam lies on the banks of the River Tay and became a place favoured by tourists after the Victorians brought the railway to that picturesque area. A short well signed path from the centre of Birnam leads to the Birnam Oak. Seen here, this ancient oak is claimed to be the only survivor of the Birnam Wood described in the Shakespeare play.

While also known as Macbeth's Oak it is highly unlikely to have existed in Macbeth's day. However, it is centuries old and was quite possibly well grown when Shakespeare is claimed to have visited Perthshire as an actor in 1589.

It is improbable that Shakespeare ever saw Birnam Wood. There is little doubt though that any forces attacking Dunsinane Hill would have had easy access to wood-like camouflage centuries earlier. If during an attack on Dunsinane, a line existed above which trees such as oak could not grow, then using such camouflage would be essential to avoid early detection during daylight hours.

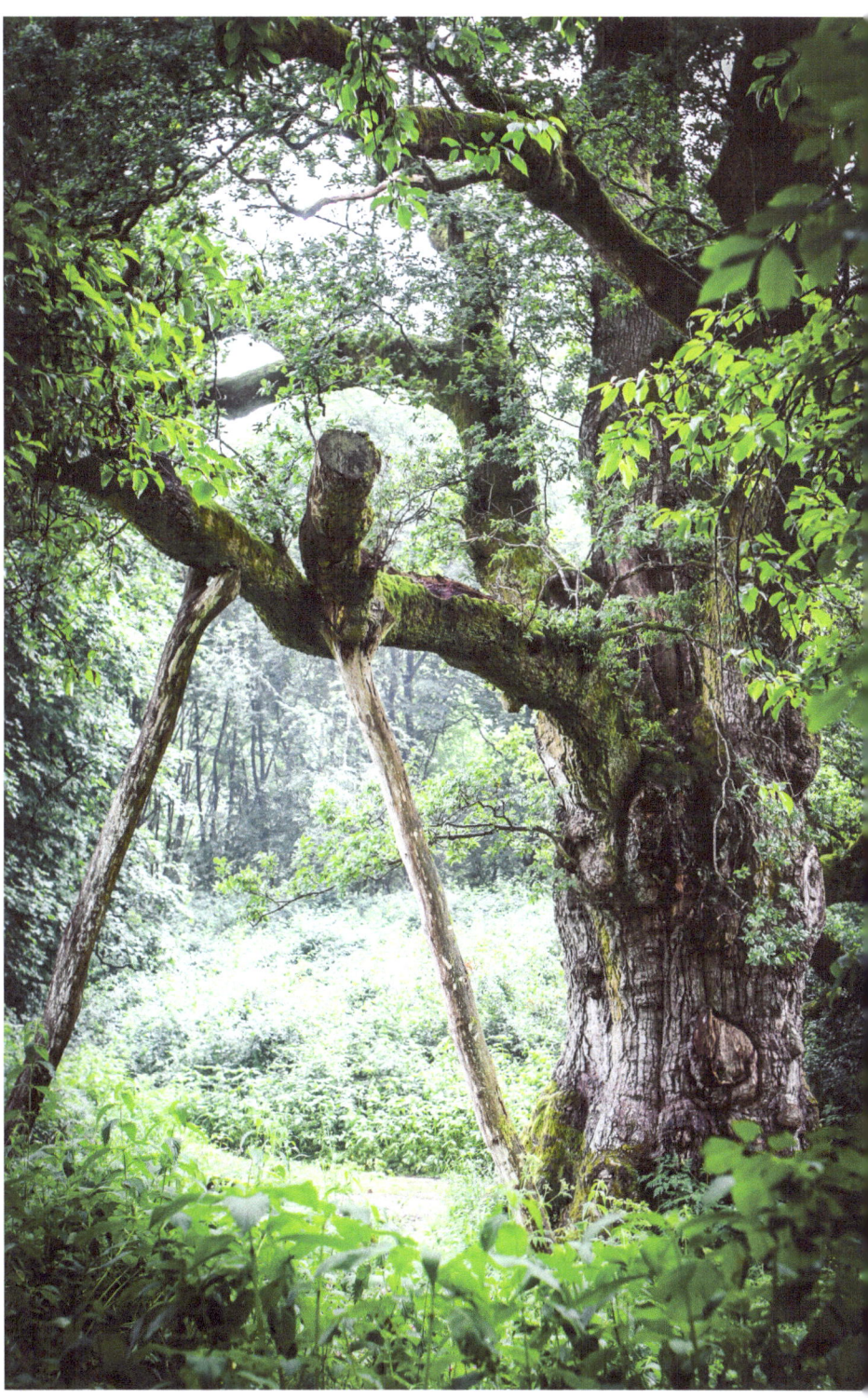

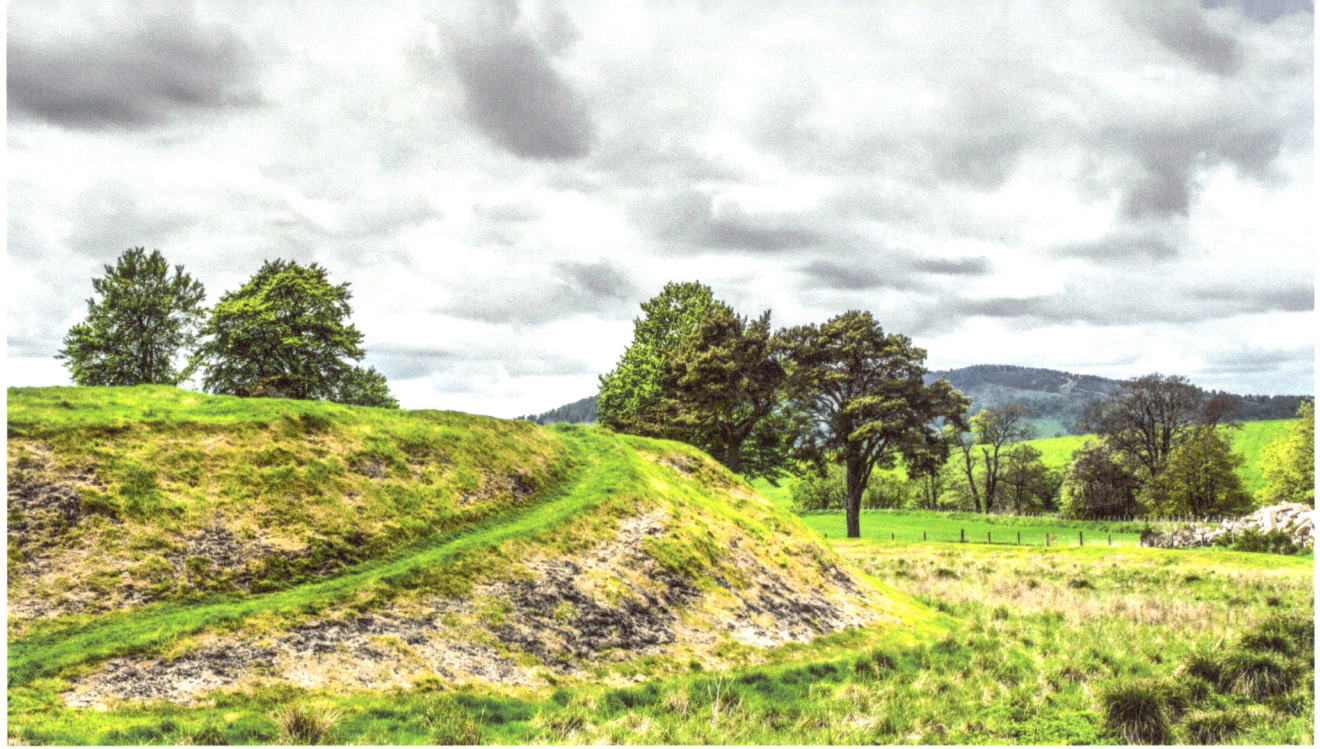

Lumphanan, Aberdeenshire

Macbeth survived as King of Scotland despite his defeat at Dunsinane by Siward, who himself died in 1055.

It has been argued that in 1057 Macbeth seems to have stepped down in favour of his stepson. Macbeth was by then quite old. It would, then, be logical for him to resign in favour of Lulach, who had probably ruled during his stepfather's pilgrimage to Rome. At the same time though, Malcolm, son of King Duncan, was intent on seizing the crown. Malcolm had married into the Norwegian Royal Family and persuaded Harold, the son of the Norwegian King, to join in an attack on Scotland. It is likely that a representative of the Earl of Fife's family sailed with the fleet out of Orkney. This is thought to have been Macduff.

King Lulach was killed when the two sides met at Essie in Aberdeenshire on 17th March 1058. Lulach's own son was too young to take the crown and stop Malcolm.

Macbeth was therefore obliged to muster remaining forces loyal to Moray against Malcolm and his Norse allies. The two armies met and fought at Lumphanan, also in Aberdeenshire, in August 1058.

The sequence, detail and timing of events in 1057 and 1058 are especially subject to historical debate. The above summary is from Fiona Watson's thoroughly researched book about Macbeth. (See Page 2)

The battle site is not signed locally nor shown on maps. However, it is likely to be in the vicinity of the Peel of Lumphanan, shown above. This is a defensive structure dating from the early 13th century. Just 300 metres from the Peel is Macbeth's Stone which is where the Undiscovered Scotland website says that Macbeth was beheaded after defeat in the battle. The stone is on farmed land but can be seen in the photograph on the opposite page. It is sited between the fence and the tree.

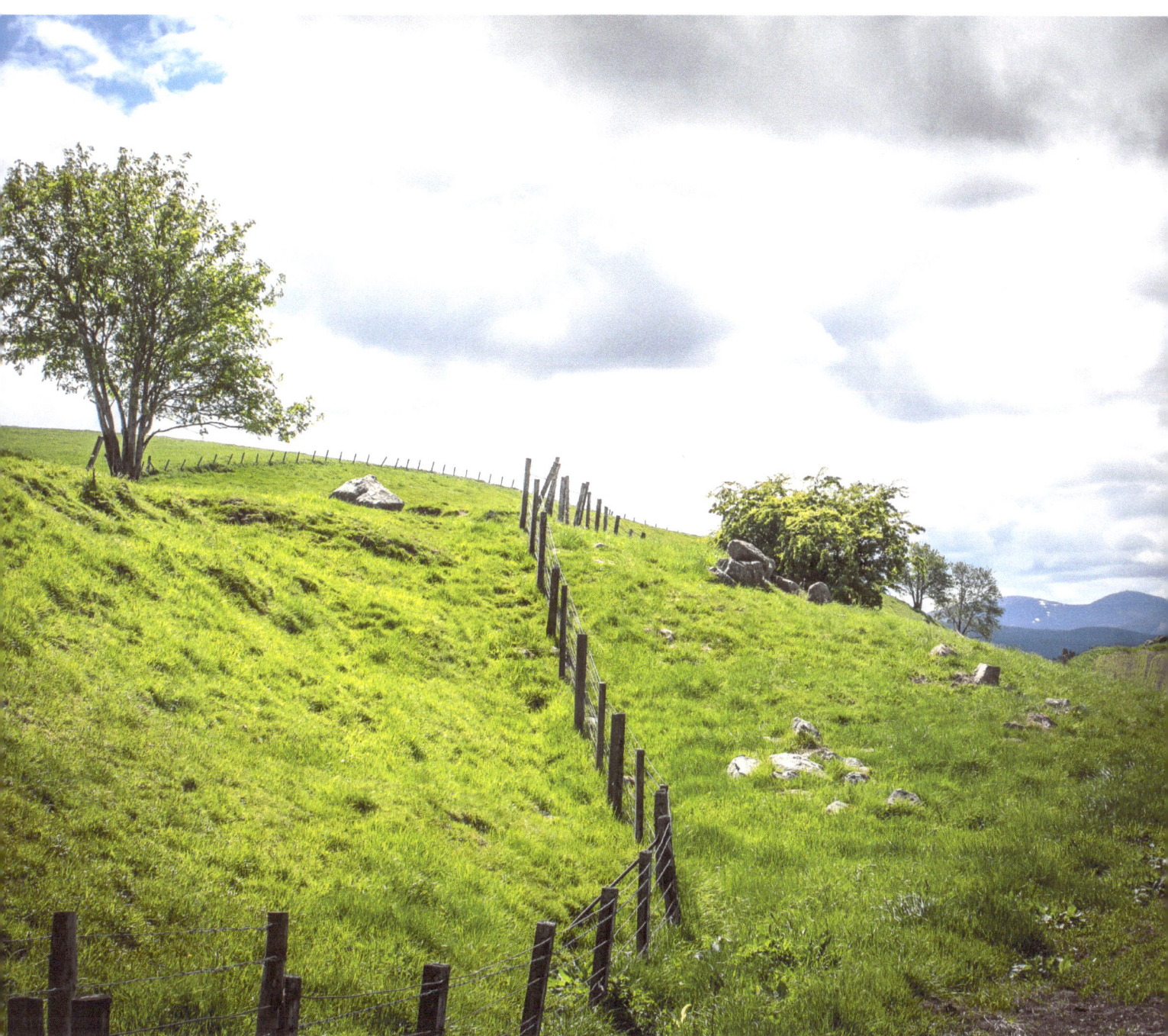

Saint Finan's Cemetery, Lumphanan

As already mentioned, there is much that is unknown about Macbeth, Son of Finlay. The Shakespeare death scene at Dunsinane at the hand of Macduff who was "none of woman born" is clearly far off the mark. However, it is the case that Malcolm, and maybe even Macduff, at least had some relevance to his demise.

The actual place and nature of Macbeth's death are obscure. It is generally accepted that there was a battle in Aberdeenshire, most probably at Lumphanan, but whether he died during combat or later from his wounds is not known.

One version of the battle says that he died of a head wound at the spot of Macbeth's Stone. Another version claims he was captured during, or after, the battle and beheaded at the same stone. That death scene seems more in keeping with the life and death of an evil Macbeth as portrayed by Holinshed and Shakespeare than that of an honourable and reasonable ex-King.

The blur between fact and fiction doesn't end with Macbeth's death. A local tale claimed he was buried in a nearby cemetery in Lumphanan. St Finan's Church was only built here in 1762, but it was on the site of earlier places of worship with foundations from the 7th and 13th centuries. The more ancient burial ground may indeed have been conveniently close to the carnage after the Battle of Lumphanan.

The church ceased to be a place of worship and was bought in the 1980's by the owners of the adjacent manse. As can be seen in the photograph here it appears to be in sound condition, complete with an intact and maintained graveyard.

While Macbeth might have been temporarily interred at the Lumphanan graveyard, it is generally believed that Malcolm had his body removed to the ancient burial ground on Iona in the Western Isles. This graveyard was the place where all proper Kings were put to rest. It contains the graves of many early Scottish, Irish, Norwegian and French Kings.

The respect and honour that Macbeth had earned, even in the eyes of Malcolm, by the time of his death is clearly indicated by the fact that his body was moved there, over 150 miles away. In the words of Fiona Watson, from her authoritative and revealing book Macbeth - A True Story; "This final act is testament to the place Macbeth occupied in Scotland at the time. Here was no tyrant, but a ruler of great skill and fortitude, a man willing and able to give his people peace and prosperity without losing either popularity or support."

And so, the final link to Macbeth in this book is not a monument recalling the dark times of the 11th century, but a family home in the 21st century complete with children's playthings and a greenhouse. This can be viewed as a vivid reminder that history lives all around us. Macbeth would be proud to see this home as a symbol of what became of the Scotland he helped to build. This graveyard is probably a far better place to remember and admire the great man than anywhere else.

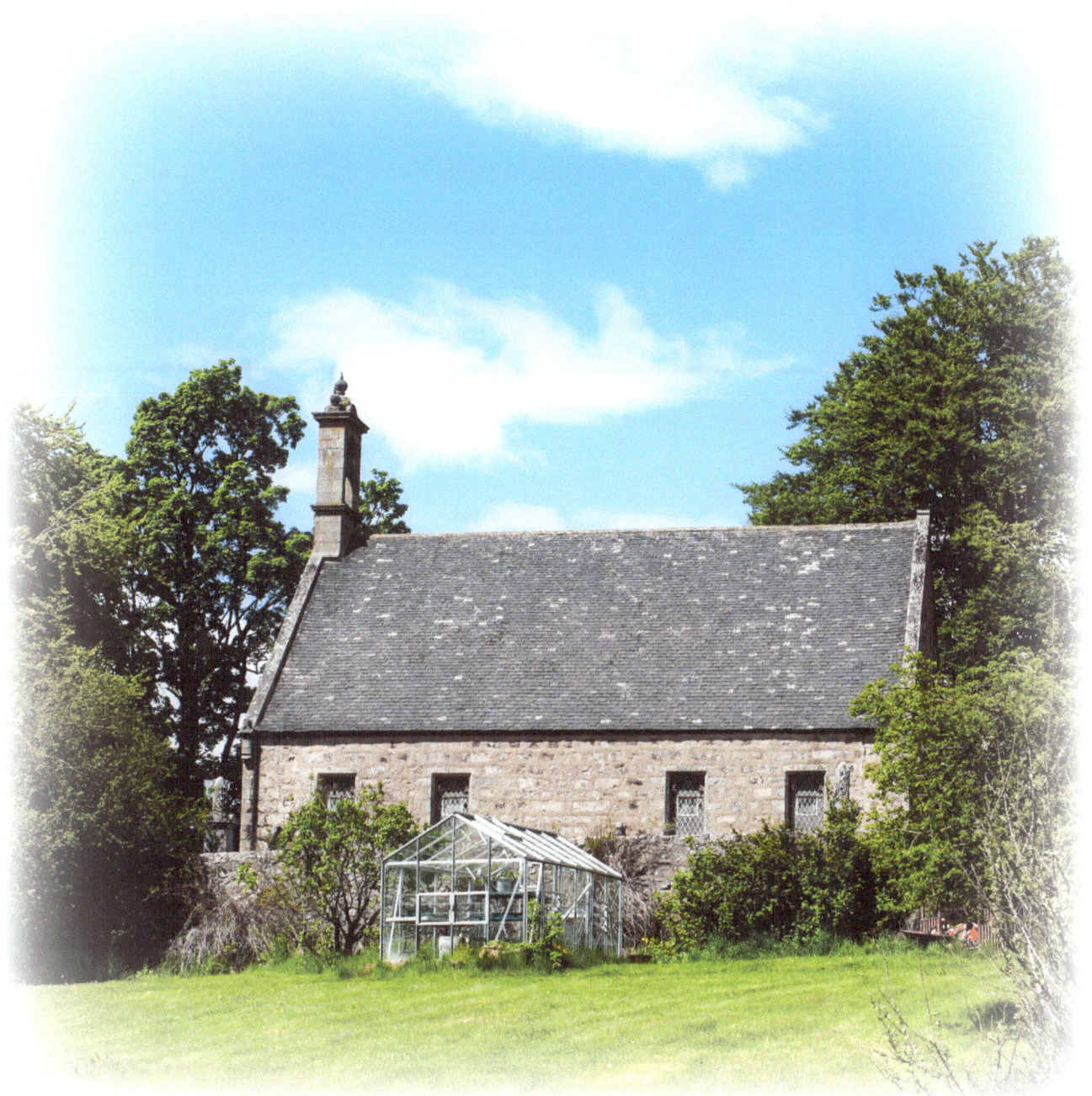

Photographer's Notes

The Camera

I've enjoyed taking photographs since I was about nine years old. Now in my sixties I must admit to owning and using more cameras than I can remember. Not being a wealthy anorak I've never owned "the best". So, in the hope that other amateur photographers on a budget out there are actually interested, I thought I'd use these pages to pass on any wisdom I believe I've gained over the years.

Some say that the best camera is the one you have with you at the time. Well I've noticed that the guys that come out with this tale also happen to own a full frame DSLR, so excuse me if I doubt their sincerity.

Film or Digital? No debate, in terms of cost and post-exposure flexibility digital wins hands down. I fully appreciate the art, skill and effort that goes into film photography. In fact, Joe Cornish is one of my heroes. However, I think you've got to be a wealthy masochist to love film photography. I too-well recall the time, leg-ache and utter misery involved in self-processing and printing 36 exposure film rolls.

After trying a modest Canon DSLR, followed by good compacts like the Canon G9, I decided to go back to DSLRs. By this time I was of the strong opinion that it was still the quality of lens that really mattered. So my next camera would be from the brand with the best lenses. Making the decision was quite difficult because lens quality has so improved recently thanks to computer aided design and manufacture. Inevitably, though, choice came down to either Nikon or Canon.

In the end I decided Nikon was the one for me. After reading lots of comparative reviews, I got the impression that Nikon lenses were considered very marginally and very generally better than Canon.

I was so committed to the best lens plan that I actually bought the lens before the camera. I traded a very under-rated Nikon P7000 compact for a barely used Nikkor 35mm F2. Pending funds to buy the camera to go with it, I used my wife's terrific Panasonic Lumix LX5 compact. The camera I eventually chose was a used Nikon D200. The pair became the best photography kit I'd ever had, and which produced the some of the best photographs I'd ever taken up to that time.

In hindsight I suspect the main reason for the pleasure and success that this kit brought me was because of its comparative simplicity. I was able to fully understand everything about it, master it and produce consistently acceptable images. During this time I did my very first wedding commission for an old friend. That D200 & 35mm Nikkor combination was just brilliant for the job...no fuss, no flash...and a pile of properly exposed and focussed photos. To this day I still love the candid shot of my friend Alan, the bride's father, with his head in his hands!

I suppose this leads to the whole point of me writing these pages, because the key wisdom I want to impart is that I fervently believe the best camera is the one you know best, are most comfortable with and which also gives consistently good results.

Imaging Software

There are many who regard the use of imaging software as cheating. I'm not one of them. Digital technology and associated software has revolutionised and extended my hobby. I would never have contemplated compiling this book without it and think the software I've used deserves a mention here.

I always try to compose my shots and get a good image in the camera but they often fail to meet my own standards. Practically all of the photos in this book have had to be adjusted in some way. After many years of dabbling I eventually tried Adobe Photoshop Lightroom. I've grown to regard it as all I really need to download, "develop", file, organise and print. Like the cameras I've used, Lightroom got better as I grew to understand it.

The new images for this book were downloaded straight into Lightroom and adjusted as required. For those interested, the most often used adjustments were cropping, tone adjustment & clarity. Sometimes though, Lightroom can't do enough if the image is correctly exposed but downright boring. I'm not the kind of photographer who can afford the patience, time or petrol to go back and try again. So, if I thought an underwhelming photo really must be included in this book, I've resorted to using a free version of Photomatix software to zap things up a bit. This is a stand-alone HDR tonemapping program which can, for example, turn a boring cloudy sky into something really moody or dramatic.

HDR-type processing is used a lot these days and is the cause of much debate among photographers. My own view was influenced when I eventually realised that a vast amount of published photographs had been so processed. So, if you can't beat them......?

Desk Top Publishing

After I started this book I thought it would be nice to use an updated version of Aldus Pagemaker, especially after my usual word-processor Libre Office failed to be up to the task.

A lot has happened to Pagemaker since I'd last used it in the late 80's. It changed names and now lives on as Adobe InDesign. I acquired a very cheap outdated copy and that is what I've used to put my book together. It took a little while to get the hang of, but eventually showed itself to be as enjoyable to use as Pagemaker ever was. InDesign can export in the PDF file format which is ideal for printing anywhere.

Some will tell you that powerful processors, lots of memory and large colour-accurate screens are essential for photo-image and DTP work. Most of that wisdom will come from well paid professionals, or those with large wallets who buy nothing but Apple. I use a modest cheap-range Toshiba laptop and no complaints at all!

Finally

That's all I want to say about camera kit & software. I don't think it will serve any great purpose to give details for every image used in this book. However, if any reader would like more information about anything at all in this book, or the equipment and software use I'd be glad to answer via e-mail: brian@lockeyb.plus.com.